DAN JENKINS'
TEXAS COLLEGE FOOTBALL LEGENDS

SAM BAUGH

Best There Ever Was

By Whit Canning

Edited by

Dan Jenkins

SPORTS

IN ASSOCIATION WITH THE

Fort Worth Star-Telegram

WESLEY R. TURNER, President and Publisher
MICHAEL BLACKMON, Vice President, Editorial Director
JACK B. TINSLEY, Vice President, Community Affairs
JIM WITT, Vice President, Executive Editor
KEVIN DALE, Managing Editor

Acknowledgements

All chapters in the "Ten to Remember" section are reprinted
by permission of the *Fort Worth Star-Telegram*. Copyright 1934, 1935, 1936 and 1937
by the *Fort Worth Star-Telegram*. All rights reserved.

Designed by Daniel J. Janke

ISBN 1-57028-174-2
ISBN (Leatherbound Edition) 1-57028-166-1

Published by

Masters Press
2647 Waterfront Parkway, East Drive
Indianapolis, Indiana 46214
317-298-5706

For other sports publications in the Masters Press library,
call toll-free 1-800-722-2677 or contact our web site at www.masterspress.com

CONTENTS

Foreword Kevin Dale iv

Introduction Dan Jenkins............................vi

Chapter One A Texas Legend 12

Chapter Two Greatest Ever 19

Chapter Three TCU Early Days....................26

Chapter Four Clash of the Titans................35

Chapter Five 1936 Season at TCU 47

Chapter Six Brush with Baseball 62

Chapter Seven A Brave New World............68

Chapter Eight A Chief Among Redskins 80

Chapter Nine A Tough Assignment 92

Chapter Ten Home on the Range 98

Chapter Eleven Baugh's Legacy 106

Ten to Remember 114

" *Dutch taught us a short passing game,
and early on he told me,
'You can throw from your own one-yard line,
if you see an opening.'
We were doing a lot of things nobody else
had thought of.* "

– Sam Baugh

Baugh & Jenkins: Two Legends

It's not often that I wish I was born earlier. OK, being a teenager in the 70's with disco music on the radio was tough. But the last four decades of the 20th century have been tolerable. Except, I never got to see Sammy Baugh throw a football.

Baugh was done with football in the 1950's. But his two decades in the game were unparalleled.

It all started in 1934 in Fort Worth at Texas Christian University. A tall kid, recruited to play baseball by then-coach Dutch Meyer, Baugh chose TCU because the Horned Frogs were going to let him play football, too.

That was the beginning of a legendary career, one that makes Baugh an easy selection for the Dan Jenkins' Texas College Football Legends series. The series will include profiles of a dozen players and coaches who have shaped college football in a state that has been producing Saturday afternoon thrills for decades.

In his second year at TCU, Baugh's baseball coach took over the football team. Meyer wanted the team to throw the ball, and Baugh was on the spot. In a time when ground attack was the favored mode of offense for football teams, Baugh and TCU tossed their way to national prominence. In 1935, the Frogs found themselves in a furious battle with LSU in the Sugar Bowl.

Though Baugh could not get the offense revved up on a cold, rainy day, he punted 14 times to keep the Tigers in poor field position. The final: 3-2, and TCU had its first national championship.

Baugh's record at TCU was 29-7-2 during three seasons. Most amazing, however, were his passing statistics. Baugh completed 270 passes for 3,384 yards and 39 touchdowns.

"Everything I learned about football, I learned from Dutch Meyer," Baugh told The Fort Worth Star-Telegram. "Back in those days, most teams — even in the pros — would only throw on third down, and then they always tried a deep pass.

"Dutch taught us a short passing game, and early on he told me, 'You can throw from your own one-yard line, if you see an opening.' We were doing a lot of things nobody else had thought of."

Truth be told, other teams would not have been as successful with the passing offense. In 1935 there was only one Sammy Baugh. Twice, he was honored as an all-America selection in college and then went on to an unforgettable professional career. Through it all, he kept his Texas roots and settled on a ranch in Rotan. Getting him off the ranch can be tough, unless there are 18 fairways and greens at the destination.

It's no surprise that Dan Jenkins would select Sammy Baugh for this series. Of course there's the talent. But add that Baugh played and won a national title for Jenkins' hometown team and his love of golf, and the selection is inescapable.

Jenkins grew up watching Baugh and saw him play in that epic duel with TCU in 1935. It began a life-long love of Southwest Conference football that manifests itself here. There were few equals to Baugh when it came to throwing a football, and there are few equals to Jenkins when it comes to writing about the sport.

The two combined are dead-solid perfect.

KEVIN DALE
Managing Editor
Fort Worth Star-Telegram

INTRODUCTION

Slingin' Sam

By Dan Jenkins

Any discussion of Slingin' Sam Baugh, the greatest passer and punter that football has ever known, invites my favorite sports trivia question, which is this: name the only three quarterbacks in history who ever led their college team to a national championship and their pro team to an NFL championship.

Sam Baugh was the first to do it, of course, or why else would I ask the question?

Samuel Adrian Baugh did it when he piloted the TCU Horned Frogs to one of the mythical national titles that were granted in 1935, after which he hurled and punted the Washington Redskins to the National Football League championships of 1937 and 1942.

The other guys? Joe Namath and Joe Montana.

It wasn't until many seasons later that Namath drove Alabama to a national crown in 1964, then performed that Super Bowl miracle for the New York Jets in the season of 1969. Montana became the third to duplicate the feat when he guided Notre Dame to No. 1 in 1977, and then as a San Francisco 49er wrapped up all those Super Bowl rings in the seasons of 1981, 1982, 1984, 1988, and 1989. Baugh, Namath, and Montana. There may not be a more exclusive club in all of football —unless it's the one in which Sam is the only member.

He appears on more all-time teams than Jim Thorpe, George Gipp, and Red Grange combined, just to pick three names at random.

It was in 1969 that *Sports Illustrated*, on the 100-year anniversary of the game, enlisted a high-level panel to select college football's all-time team, the "Eleven Best Eleven" from the entire century. The result was:

QB — **Sam Baugh, TCU, 1934-35-36.**
HB — Red Grange, Illinois, 1923-24-25.
HB — Doak Walker, SMU, 1947-48-49.

FB — O. J. Simpson, USC, 1967-68.
E — Don Hutson, Alabama, 1933-34.
E — Bennie Oosterbaan, Michigan, 1925-26-27.
T — George Connor, Notre Dame, 1946-47.
T — Bronko Nagurski, Minnesota, 1928-29.
G — Bob Suffridge, Tennessee, 1938-39-40.
G — Tommy Nobis, Texas, 1963-64-65.
O — Robert Peck, Pittsburgh, 1915-16.

It was in 1991, likewise, that ESPN-TV conducted a poll of more than 300 sportswriters and sportscasters to select the all-time top 22 players in the entire history of college football. That result was:

QB — **Sam Baugh, TCU, 1934-35-36.**
      Roger Stauback, Navy, 1963-64.
HB — Red Grange, Illinois, 1923-24-25.
      Doak Walker, SMU, 1947-48-49.
      Tom Harmon, Michigan, 1939-40.
      Tony Dorsett, Pittsburgh, 1974-75-76.
FB — Herschel Walker, Georgia, 1980-81-82.
      O. J. Simpson, USC, 1967-68.
E — Don Hutson, Alabama, 1933-34.
      Bennie Oosterbaan, Michigan, 1925-26-27.
      Johnny Rodgers, Nebraska, 1970-71-72.
      Anthony Carter, Michigan, 1981-82.
T — **Bob Lilly, TCU, 1958-59-60.**
      Lee Roy Selmon, Oklahoma, 1974-75.
      George Connor, Notre Dame, 1946-47.
      Bronko Nagurski, Minnesota, 1928-29.
G — Bob Suffridge, Tennessee, 1938-39-40.
      Jim Parker, Ohio State, 1954-55-56.
      Tommy Nobis, Texas, 1963-64-65.
      John Hannah, Alabama, 1971-72.
C — Dick Butkus, Illinois, 1963-64.
      David Rimington, Nebraska, 1981-82.

You may notice Bob Lilly's name highlighted. As a TCU grad myself, I wouldn't want it overlooked — and I think Sam would join me in this — that TCU is one of only five schools to have two players selected.

Likewise again, it was in 1995 that a noted panel chose the all-time NFL team of the past 75 seasons. Here were the selections on offense:

QB — **Sam Baugh, Washington Redskins** (TCU)
       Otto Graham, Cleveland Browns
       (Northwestern)
       Joe Montana, San Francisco 49ers
       (Notre Dame)
       Johnny Unitas, Baltimore Colts (Louisville)
RB — Jim Brown, Cleveland Browns (Syracuse)
       Marion Motley, Cleveland Browns
       (Nevada-Reno)
       Bronko Nagurski, Chicago Bears (Minnesota)
       Walter Payton, Chicago Bears (Jackson State)
       Gale Sayers, Chicago Bears (Kansas)
       O. J. Simpson, Buffalo Bills (USC)
       Steve Van Buren, Philadelphia Eagles (LSU)
WR —Lance Alworth, San Diego Chargers
       (Arkansas)
       Raymond Berry, Baltimore Colts (SMU)
       Don Hutson, Green Bay Packers (Alabama)
       Jerry Rice, San Francisco 49ers,
       (Miss. Valley State)
TE — Mike Ditka, Chicago Bears (Pittsburgh)
       Kellen Winslow, San Diego Chargers
       (Missouri)
T —   Rosey Brown, N.Y. Giants (Morgan State)
       Forrest Gregg, Green Bay Packers (SMU)
       Anthony Munoz, Cincinnati Bengals (USC)
G —   John Hannah, New England Patriots
       (Alabama)
       Jim Parker, Baltimore Colts (Ohio State)
       Gene Upshaw, Oakland Raiders (Texas A&I)
C —   Mel Hein, N.Y. Giants (Washington State)
       Mike Webster, Pittsburgh Steelers
       (Wisconsin)

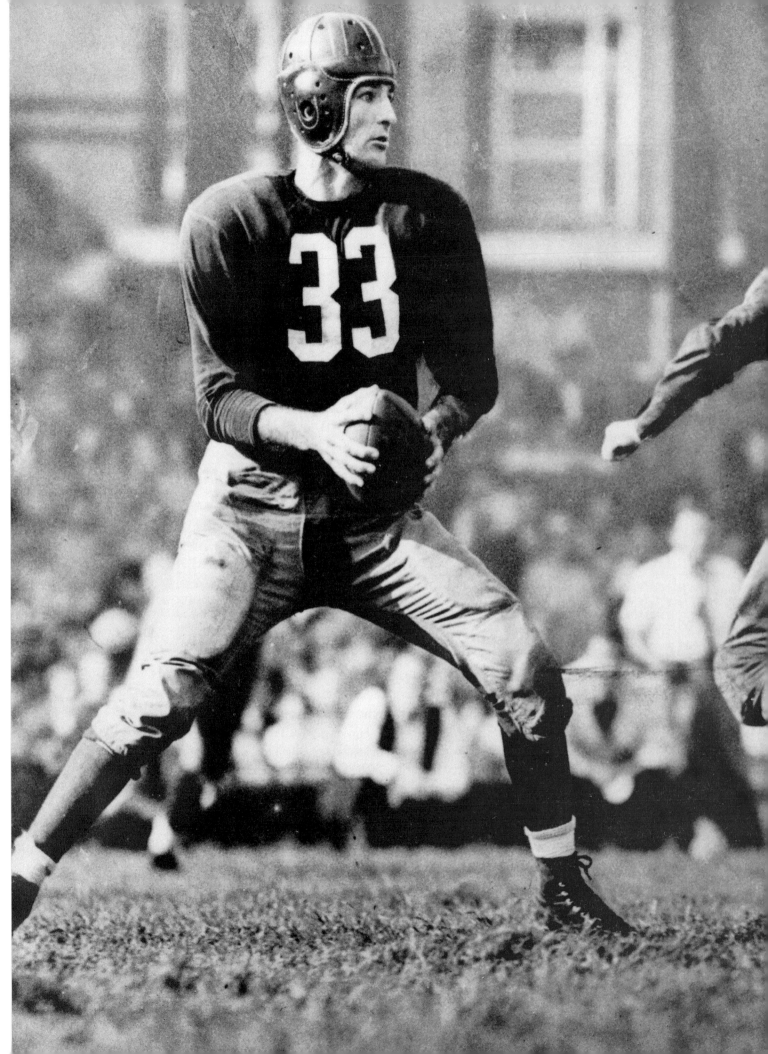

'A Texas Legend'

CHAPTER ONE

Record-Setting Rancher

Sam Baugh's Exploits Produce National Attention for the Young SWC

In the summer of 1994, after it had become painfully and indelibly certain that the Southwest Conference would soon become just another octogenarian trampled beneath the boots of progress, a sort of panicky afterthought began to emerge.

It occurred to the remaining minions of the doomed league that through all the years of stunning triumphs, amid legions of glittering all-Americans and a final, agonizing collapse, something had been forgotten: no one had ever thought to establish a SWC Hall of Fame.

They sought to correct the oversight with an inaugural class of inductees that would stand forever as a glowing symbol of what the SWC was, at its best.

Their gaze fell naturally upon five men — Davey O'Brien, Doak Walker, John David Crow, Earl Campbell and Andre Ware — who at various points in history had managed to grasp college football's brass ring: the Heisman Trophy.

And so, when the first official group of SWC immortals was announced at the annual Kickoff Luncheon in Dallas in late August, the honoree class consisted of those five distinguished alumni.

And Sam Baugh.

Although Baugh never won a Heisman — the award wasn't even in existence until his junior year at TCU — inaugurating an SWC Hall of Fame without him would have been akin to discussing the development of agriculture without mentioning the plow.

The first time the outside world sat up and noticed the wild and woolly league in Texas, it was largely due to Baugh's proficiency with the forward pass, in a revolutionary offense dreamed up by a coach named Dutch Meyer.

And after the cream of the sporting press — led by the famed Grantland Rice — witnessed a mesmerizing showdown of unbeatens (TCU and SMU) in Fort Worth in 1935, the SWC was granted a long and illustrious life.

At the end of that life, mourners gathered to honor those who had made it illustrious — including an 80-year-old rancher who seemed to have won just about everything (except a Heisman Trophy).

So when Baugh walked into the lobby of Dallas' Reunion Hyatt on a scorching late summer morning, he was greeted by a microphone and a query wondering how he felt, being included in this esteemed circle.

"Like a bastard at a family reunion," said Slingin' Sam.

A line delivered from the hip, as straight as the West Texas highway that brought Baugh to Dallas for the occasion. On the way, he stopped in Fort Worth to pick up some old pals — Allie White, Walter Roach (both now deceased) and Melvin Diggs.

When approaching any large city, one must be assured of familiar and affable company, and Baugh regards any township boasting a freeway with extreme suspicion.

Arriving for the occasion, the boys sailed past the exit ramp and were eventually obliged to execute a U-turn to reach the Hyatt. Baugh dutifully apologized to the luncheon crowd for their tardiness, explaining that "We don't have this problem in Rotan (population 1,913)."

A towering, rail-thin figure in boots and Stetson hat, he stood on the podium and told the guests that it was kind of a damn shame that a great conference had to die because a few people couldn't stop bickering long enough to save it.

Then the weathered face crinkled into a smile, and he soon had them rolling in the aisles with tales of Wee

Willie Wilkin, his free-spirited comrade-in-arms with the Washington Redskins.

All in all, it was a rather long affair, with a great number of speakers. But at the end of the day, they were sad to see Sam Baugh go.

EASY-GOING NATURE

A typical performance, says his son David, who was present at a similar occasion about a year later when the main street in Rotan was renamed in honor of his father.

"They did it in the middle of the summer, and had this ceremony in the town square," David says, laughing. "Then they asked Sam to make a speech.

"So he gets up and says, 'Well, it's hotter than hell out here, and I know all of y'all got better things to do, so I'm not gonna keep you any longer.' "

Indicating that he had been perfectly satisfied with the street when it was called Snyder Avenue, Baugh then made an alternate suggestion.

"There was a couple of school teacher sisters," Baugh says, "who taught everybody who ever grew up in this town for about 40 years, and I just said that if they had to rename it, they ought to rename it after them.

"I've never done anything for Rotan."

Nevertheless, David recalls, "we were there about another hour, because just about everyone in town came up and asked Sam for his autograph."

Now 83, Baugh spends most of his time playing golf and avoiding fanfare. Over the years he has done the latter so well that it has been easy to overlook the reasons why so many want his autograph.

"I guess, frankly, that for most of my life I've thought of Sam more as a rancher," says David, who now manages the family ranch and coaches the football team in Snyder. "Because around here, that's what he was.

"Every once in awhile, though, something comes up that kind of makes you look at his record, and it's pretty amazing.

"A couple of years ago, the National Football League named him to their 75th anniversary team, and that was impressive. They put out a book on it, and it was a real nice deal."

But with Baugh, flattery will get you only so far.

"The Redskins have been trying for years to get him up there so they can have a 'Sam Baugh Day' and a big presentation and retire his jersey," David says. "But he'll never go.

"Jack Kent Cooke offered several times to have a private jet flown in here, send a limo out to the ranch to pick up Sam, fly him to Washington and put him up, and they bring him back after the ceremony."

It's a nice thought, but in his 83rd year, Baugh is still trying to figure out why anyone would actually go to a city, if they didn't have to.

"I haven't been back to that place since I retired in 1952," he says. "I coached in New York a few years later, but I hated it so much I just about never left the apartment except to go to work.

"Besides, nowadays, I don't like to be anywhere where I can't get home by dark."

RECORDS STILL STAND

At TCU, where he guided the Frogs to a 29-7-2 record, two bowl victories and part of a mythical national championship, Baugh completed 270 passes for 3,384 yards and 39 touchdowns in three years — record-setting numbers for that day and time. He also averaged 41.3 yards on 198 punts and, most times, played a full game on defense.

When Baugh took his expertise to the NFL, he led Washington to a title as a rookie and was immediately hailed as a man who had revolutionized the game with his amazing passing ability.

In reality, he says, "TCU's offense at the time was much more sophisticated than anything they had in pro ball — and I just started putting those plays into the Washington offense.

In 16 seasons at Washington, he guided the Redskins to five title games and two NFL championships while leading the league in passing six times, punting four times and interceptions (from his defensive safety position) once.

He established a large collection of records for the time. Some, amazingly, are still standing.

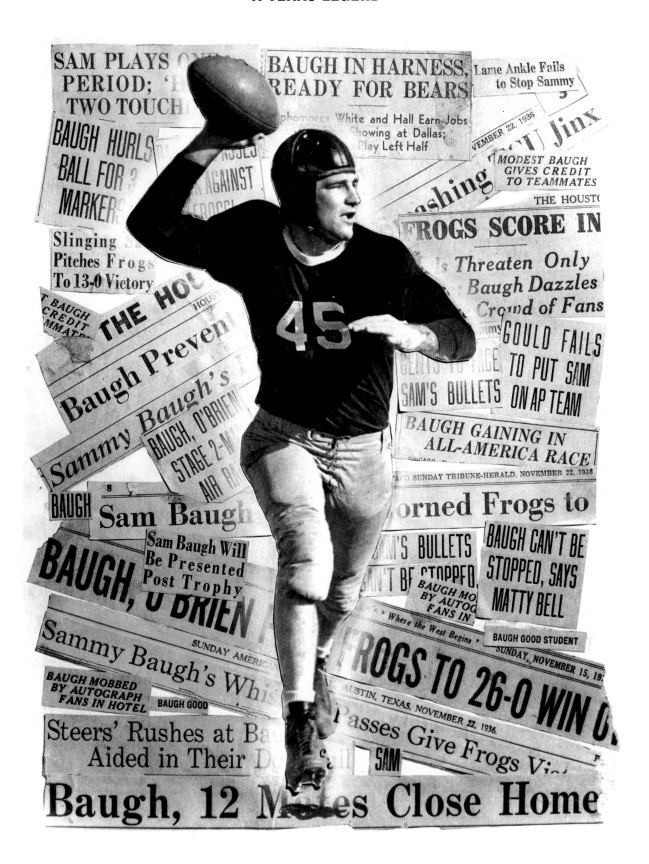

The all-time NFL record for best punting average in a season is 51.4 yards. Baugh set it 57 years ago, and he's also still the best punter in NFL history, with a 45.1 career average.

He still holds the Washington record for career touchdown passes with 187, and his career passing yardage — 22,085 — ranks third behind Joe Theismann (25,206) and Sonny Jurgensen (22,585). As a defensive back he intercepted 31 passes — third on the Redskins' career list behind Darrell Green (40) and Brig Owens (36). He once threw for 446 yards in a game — still a Washington record.

He is a charter (1963) member of the NFL Hall of Fame and holds at least one record that could stand for centuries: in a 42-20 victory over Detroit on November 14, 1943, he threw four touchdown passes — and intercepted four from the Lions.

"The way the game is played today," he says, with a twinkle in the eye, "I don't think that one will ever be broken."

In view of the sweeping significance of all this, Baugh had given careful thought over the years to the way in which he would like his achievements framed for posterity.

"He has told me," David says, "that on his tombstone, he would kinda like it to say: 'Pretty Good Cowman.'"

Reluctant hero: Sam Baugh accepts his place in the College Football Hall of Fame in 1951. He was also inducted into the Pro Football Hall of Fame in 1963.

CHAPTER TWO

'He Was the Greatest I Ever Saw'

Even as a Youth, Baugh Impressed Coaches, Teammates Alike With His Uncanny Skills

When Samuel Adrian Baugh was born in a farmhouse near Temple, Texas, on March 17, 1914, the idea that he would one day become legendary in a business called professional football would have been comparable to a notion that he would someday be the head of NASA.

At that time, professional football did not exist, and two-seat, prop-driven aircraft — never mind rockets to the moon — were still widely regarded as suspicious contraptions piloted by idiots.

There was football — a game, played by some collegians, with no apparent purpose other than to get everyone covered with mud down at the bottom of an amorphous pile of bodies. It seemed about as pointless as that silly war they were soon fighting in Europe because some Austrian archduke got himself shot.

The opiate of the masses was baseball — a marvelously subtle contest of skill that made heroes out of resourceful characters like Ty Cobb and John McGraw. And out on the farm, even that was something you paid little attention to until the work was done.

Waiting 15 years down the road was a terrible crash that plunged the nation into The Great Depression, but for awhile, rural life in central Texas was almost idyllic.

"We lived out there on that farm when I was little — six miles out of town — and I really loved that life," Baugh says. "We had a few diary cows, and living out there in the country — just doin' the chores and not worrying much about anything else, seemed like the perfect way to go through life.

"But when I was about 5 or 6, we moved into town because my daddy got a job with the Santa Fe Railroad. So I actually grew up — most of the way — in Temple."

By the time high school approached, it was obvious that the farm boy — rapidly growing toward an eventual height of 6-foot-2 — was a natural athlete adept at just about any sport that was in season. During his first year at Temple High, he was a year-round star in football, basketball and baseball.

"That first year," he says, laughing, "I played on just about the sorriest football team Temple ever had — and one of the best basketball teams.

"I was a pretty tall kid even then — but we had two other guys who were a lot bigger than me — about 6-5 — so we won a lot of basketball games. A couple of years later, in fact, those guys won a state championship, but by then I was gone."

The football team was a different story.

"God, we were just pretty awful," Baugh says. "I played end — which was where they had always put me all through junior high because I was tall. But I also had a pretty strong arm.

"One day the coach, Bill Henderson, came around and said,

Dutch Meyer recruited Sam Baugh to play both football and baseball for TCU.

19

Bullseye: Baugh practices his accurate passing skills while at his parent's home in West Texas.

'I'm putting you back there at tailback (quarterback), because you're the only guy on the team who can throw the ball. We're not ever gonna be able to stop anybody, but maybe we can get 'em confused by throwing the ball.'

"I said, 'Well, it's fine with me. Whatever you think.'

"But it never made a damn bit of difference as far as I could see, because we went ahead and lost the rest of our games, anyway."

Unfortunately for the Wildcats, however, the Baugh family fortunes were soon in a state of flux.

"By then it was the Depression," Baugh says, "and a lot of people were out of work, looking for work, or changing jobs or where they lived.

"My daddy got bumped by someone with more seniority, and lost his job in Temple, so he bumped somebody in Somerville and the family moved over there. Then he bumped somebody else in Sweetwater, and we moved out there. Nobody had any money, and if you just had a job you were ahead of a lot of people. So you went wherever the jobs were."

Meanwhile, there was a scheme afoot to keep the talented athlete in Temple, regardless of where the rest of Baughs wound up.

"One day the coach called the team together and told 'em to vote for me for captain, hoping I would stay there and live with my grandmother," Baugh says. "But my folks were not inclined to go along with that."

REMEMBERING KI ALDRICH

Although the Baughs headed west, young Sam never forgot the farm that had been his first home. And he never forgot Ki Aldrich.

"Ki was a couple of years younger than me," Baugh says, "and we lived across the street from each other in Temple. And God Almighty, how he loved to play football.

"I played that game for more than 20 years — in Temple, in Sweetwater, at TCU and in the pros — and in all those years I never saw anyone play football like Ki Aldrich. I never saw anyone who loved it like he did.

"When I was at Temple, I would come home from practice pretty worn out, but not Ki. You'd come back to the house, and in a few minutes you'd hear the noise start up.

"It would be Ki, out in their garage. He came home every day and spent the time before supper toughening himself up by going out there and banging into the garage. He would do it again and again — just slam into those boards until they called him for supper.

"They had a bunch of tin hanging in the garage — hub caps or whatever — and every time Ki hit those boards, that tin would rattle and make a big racket that you could hear for blocks."

The two were reunited a few years later when Baugh was a senior at TCU and Aldrich — a two-way center in the game of the 30's — a rather startling sophomore.

"Ki made a real quick impression when he got to the varsity at TCU," Baugh says, laughing. "He'd be out there runnin' around all over the place, running across the field and banging into people, and everyone was standin' around saying, 'Who the hell is that? And I'd say, 'Aw, that's just my buddy Ki — he's a little crazy, but you're gonna like him.' "

Two years later, Aldrich was a consensus all-American on a team — led by Davey O'Brien — that became the first consensus national champion in Southwest Conference history.

When the Baughs moved to Sweetwater, Sam found what he regarded as his true calling — baseball. He also began to develop a deep, intense love for West Texas that will last until they bury him in it.

He also played football successfully — but without spectacular notice.

"There's been some stuff written from time to time about how when I was in high school I led the Sweetwater Mustangs to the state playoffs," he says. "But it just ain't true. Hell, I was a long way from being the guy who led us to the playoffs.

"The star of that team was Red Sheridan, the tailback — and he was a whole lot better than I was. I was usually the blocking back or wingback, and I played pretty well on defense.

"But in my last season there (1932) we did have a real good team, and went to the playoffs. Our big game that year was against Big Spring — which was averaging about 40 points a game and was probably the best high school team I ever saw.

"They were real big and real fast, and nobody thought we could beat 'em, and I have to admit, it looked pretty darn near impossible. But Red had a great game and we won the district championship.

"The next week, we went up and played Amarillo in a blizzard and lost, 7-0, and that was the end of the season."

MEETING DUTCH MEYER

Baugh was unsure at the time whether or not he would ever play football again, although it was not necessarily a major concern. Baseball was still his first love, and over the years his skills had steadily improved.

By the time his senior football year was over, he had become a good enough third baseman to land a job with a local town team composed mainly of older, more experienced players.

And in the spring of 1933, a chance meeting occurred in Sweetwater that would forever alter Baugh's life — not to mention the subsequent history of Texas Christian University, the Southwest Conference, and the National Football League.

"I was playing on a town team, and we were playing games against a lot of clubs just traveling through," Baugh says. "One day, the TCU baseball team came in to play us a couple of games, and that's the first time I ever saw Dutch Meyer.

"It's funny — I had actually heard of TCU, but only because there was a teacher at Sweetwater who came from there and was always telling us what a good school it was. I can't call his name now — everyone just called him 'Froggie.' "

It was also the first time Meyer had laid eyes on Baugh, although he was aware that he had played football at Sweetwater. At the time, Meyer was TCU's freshman football coach, as well as being the head coach in basketball and baseball, and was always looking for good athletes .

L.D. Meyer was a popular target of Sam Baugh's passes while at TCU. Meyer later played professional baseball.

What he mainly figured he had discovered during that two-game series was his future third baseman. But he told Baugh that if he would come to TCU, head football coach Francis Schmidt would also be happy to give him a tryout.

But Meyer was not the only college coach interested in Sam Baugh, third baseman.

"I got a call from Uncle Billy Disch down at the University of Texas, and he said he wanted me to come down there and play for them," Baugh says. "Frankly, I was real interested, because they had a lot of supporters out around Sweetwater who had told me all about the place.

"So it was arranged for me to go down there and visit, and after seeing the campus and talking to people there, I had really just about made up my mind to go there.

"But when I asked Uncle Billy about playing football, he told me that if I came to Texas, it would have to be for baseball only.

"Well, I told him I would have to think about it. So I took a walk around the campus, just trying to think things over, and I wandered over to the stadium where the football team was practicing.

"They had a lot of well-known players and were expecting to have a real good team. So I sat down in the stands to watch for awhile.

"Sitting there watching them, I realized how much I was going to miss football.

"So I called Dutch and told him I wanted to come to TCU. I told Uncle Billy, and he was very understanding about it. In fact, he loaned me the money to get up to Fort Worth."

And so, a fortunate convergence occurred — a lanky kid from West Texas and a banty rooster of a coach, joined together by fate and destined to launch their careers together in 1934 when Schmidt took the Ohio State job.

For Baugh, who figures that "there weren't four people in Sweetwater who had a chance to go to college," it was an opportunity for which he has been unfailingly grateful through the years.

For Meyer, it was like having Excalibur thrust into his hand, but the field of stirring triumphs and dragons slain would be the gridiron, not the baseball diamond.

Dutch Meyer (left) and TCU assistant Mike Brumbelow.

WINNING OVER 'LITTLE DUTCH'

Coming in with Baugh in that freshman class in 1933 was a young man particularly well-situated to observe the phenomenon that unfolded over the next four years. In fact, he spent much of that period living in the house of the head coach, who happened to be his uncle.

His name was L.D. Meyer, and he was soon widely known as "Little Dutch."

He would one day play baseball in the major leagues, but first he would take a wild, four-year ride with the Horned Frogs during which Baugh — and Meyer's uncle — would transform a small, financially strapped school few had ever heard of into a famed national power.

"I always owed a lot to my aunt and uncle," Meyer says. "I grew up in Waco — Dutch was my dad's brother — and like almost everyone else back then, we didn't have much money.

"I had played football in high school, but nobody really recruited me. I was a pretty good end, but I wasn't real big, and I was always more interested in baseball.

"But Dutch told me to come on up to TCU — that he'd get me in school — so that's what I did. Really, we kinda snuck me into school, but nobody said anything, so I stayed.

"I lived with my aunt and uncle, and they were like surrogate parents to me. Well, particularly, my aunt was like a mother to me. Dutch was a great guy, but it was hard to separate football from the rest of his life, because football was his life.

"He always loved football and TCU, which was where he had gone to school himself. And for the rest of his life, he loved Sam Baugh."

But, Meyer says, in the beginning, his uncle had no real idea what he had.

"Dutch had seen Sam play baseball," he says. "He had heard about him playing football, but what he mostly knew about that was that Sam was supposed to be a good punter. He figured if nothing else he could be of use in that respect, and I think that's about what he told Schmidt.

"Basically, Dutch was counting on him for the baseball team, and that's the way things stood until about the middle of our first semester.

"By that time, all the coaches realized that the best passing arm in school belonged to some freshman who had been a blocking back in high school."

Although Baugh had a wonderful arm, he still wasn't quite sure what he was doing with it.

"Everything I ever learned about football, I learned from Dutch Meyer," Baugh says. "Back in those days, nobody knew anything about the passing game. Most teams — even in the pros — would try to pound at you with the running game and then, in desperation, throw on third and long. Then they would just try to throw it as far as they could.

"Dutch taught us the short passing game, and it was a revolutionary thing for that day and time. We would just move the ball right down the field hitting short passes — with little risk of an interception — and nobody could figure out how to stop it.

"Early on, he told me, 'You can throw from our one-yard line, if you see an opening, and I'll never question

> *"Everything I ever learned about football, I learned from Dutch Meyer."*
>
> *— Sam Baugh*

you.' In a lot of ways, he was years ahead of his time.

"I watch the TV today, and I see 'em doing things they think are new concepts. And they're doin' the same damn thing Dutch was doing in the 30's."

While the concepts were sound, the passing game did not suffer from having a quarterback who could hit any moving target, at any speed, anywhere on the field, chest high, with the greatest ball L.D. Meyer ever saw.

"In those days," Meyer says, "he was the greatest passer I ever saw. And in all the years since, I don't remember ever seeing anyone better. In all my life, I never saw another passer like Sam Baugh.

"Sam could throw any kind of ball — off balance or whatever — and he could throw long, short or medium. But he threw a very light ball. Most of Sam's passes, you could catch 'em with one hand."

There was one famous exception — in the titanic struggle with SMU in 1935, when a squeezed-in defense forced Baugh to rifle shots through the gaps, with the result that TCU suffered several drops and lost the game. It is a judgment Meyer does not buy.

"When the quarterback hits you square in the chest with the ball," he says, "you're supposed to catch it.

"He was the greatest I ever saw. But as good as he was throwing the ball, he was an even better punter. There was no spot on a football field where he could not drop a punt on a dime if he wanted to. I don't know how many balls I saw him put right on the sideline chalk — where there was no way you could run it back — or how many perfect 'coffin corner' kicks he made.

Meyer recalls that the quarterback who followed Baugh seemed cut from the same mold — although seven inches shorter.

"Davey (O'Brien) also threw that light ball that you could always catch," he says. "They were very much like each other — modest, unassuming, down to earth — and yet very confident of what they were doing. Both were great defensive backs, and just great athletes. And great people.

"Whatever it took to save the day, Sam or Davey could usually do it. TCU was very fortunate to have both of them."

CHAPTER THREE

The Early, Lean Times of TCU Football

When Ed Pritchard arrived on the campus of Texas Christian University in the fall of 1933, the first person he met was Sam Baugh. "We had just moved here from Eastland," says Pritchard, now a semi-retired Fort Worth businessman, "because my father had relocated his business here, and I was going to enroll at the university.

"We had found an apartment over there on the corner of Park Hill and University Drive, just a few blocks from TCU.

"One Saturday after we had gotten moved in and settled, I decided to walk up to the campus for a look around. Freshmen were scheduled to enroll the following Monday, so I figured I'd go look the place over and get my bearings.

"So I was up there walking around, and the only soul I saw was this big, tall, lanky fellow who looked about as lost and confused as I was. I went over and introduced myself, and that's how I met Sam Baugh."

The following Monday, about 100 or so Depression-era teenagers gathered at the TCU chapel to sign up for what they hoped would be the great adventure of their lives — and the first step toward a better world. For most, it was indeed that.

"It was very different world then, and TCU was much smaller, of course, than it is now," Pritchard says. "There were just a few buildings, and about 600 to 700 students.

"Actually, TCU was pretty much a West Texas school back then — that's where a great many of the students came from, and it was a place very much to my liking. I had no trouble fitting right in.

"There was a very friendly attitude, and those of us who went to school there were almost like a great big family rather than a campus full of students. You knew just about everyone in the whole school, and when you walked across the campus you greeted everyone by their first name.

"There were a few clubs, but no fraternities or sororities. With most school activities, everyone was involved. One day not long after school started, I got elected to some kind of office — I don't remember what it was — and pretty soon I was also a cheerleader.

"The main thing, I guess, was just that we were all good friends and really cared about each other. In that day and time there wasn't much money around and not many had a chance to go to college.

"We all considered TCU to be a great step forward."

ATTENDING COLLEGE ON CREDIT

At the time, the country was also attempting to take a great step forward out of the Depression, in the first year of what would prove to be a lengthy stay in the White House for Franklin Delano Roosevelt.

But at TCU, the economic savior was Pete Wright, the business manager.

"It's a fact that not many people are aware of," says L.D. Meyer, one of Baugh's teammates, "but the school nearly had to shut down back then — they almost closed the doors.

"Like almost every other individual or institution back then, TCU was going through a difficult time. The two men who saved it were Dan Rogers and Pete Wright.

"Rogers was a banker who was a great supporter of the school and helped keep TCU afloat financially. Wright was the business manager who guided the school through a very difficult period."

In Pritchard's recollection, Wright at least guided a great many young people into an opportunity they could never have afforded otherwise.

"We were almost all poor kids," he says. "I think I knew one boy who had a car, and I walked to school every day — but of course, it was just a few blocks.

"At that time, those who wanted to live on campus could get tuition, books, a room, three meals a day and a great education for something like $33 a month. But it was a lot more money than most of us had.

"So when we went in for registration, almost every kid went to Mr. Wright and said the same thing — 'I don't have any money, but I want to go to school.'

"So Mr. Wright would let you sign a note for it. And I would be willing to bet that every kid who signed one of those notes eventually paid back every penny of it, gratefully."

Baugh says that at the time, he was unaware that the school was in such desperate straits.

"But a long time later," he says, "I heard the story that one day, Pete Wright had gone downtown to meet a wealthy oilman who wrote him a check for $25,000 to keep the school afloat."

Although Pritchard did not consider himself well off at the time, he was heir to a growing family business that has done well for more than 60 years.

"My father was a lawyer over in Eastland, and eventually became the county judge," he says. "About 1926 he got the idea that oil companies should be taxed for their income, and eventually it became a law. So my father went into business figuring the taxes for various clients in the oil business out around Ranger and Eastland.

"By 1932, he had moved his business to Fort Worth, but we lived in Eastland for one more year so I could finish high school. After I graduated, we packed everything up and rode the Sunshine Special into Fort Worth, and we've been here ever since, and we're still in the same business.

"When we moved here in 1933, we were certainly not wealthy, but a couple of years later the oil business started booming, and things got a lot easier for us."

Before the boom, life was harder — but certainly bearable.

"Nobody had any money at TCU — especially the boys," Pritchard says. "Some of the girls had a little money because they came from families that could afford to send

them to college, whereas a lot of the boys were working their way through. Practically everyone was waiting tables or doing odd jobs or finding some way to help make ends meet.

"But the girls were always very understanding about it, and very cooperative. Usually, if you asked a girl out on a date, she would insist it be Dutch Treat so she would pay her own way. And in that way, she was helping the boy out.

"But everything was so cheap then that you could go out on a date for 50 cents. For a few pennies you could ride the streetcar downtown to the Worth or Hollywood theater, and then the two of you could watch the movie for 10 cents apiece.

"Then you could ride the streetcar back out to the school and finish up the night at the drugstore having a soda. So there was always a pretty lively social life."

There were also some pretty lively rules governing said social life, enforced by ever-vigilant chaperones.

"I remember in my freshman year, we didn't have a prom," Pritchard says, "because at that time, dancing was not allowed at TCU.

"But we did have something that was kind of a substitute for the usual dances. I forget what they called it, but it was held, I think, at the library, and you would fill out a card with names on it — just like a dance card.

"Instead of dancing, you would walk the girl around the building and talk. You could also hold her hand ... but you couldn't squeeze it."

"Instead of dancing, you would walk the girl around the building and talk. You could also hold her hand ... but you couldn't squeeze it."

—Sam Baugh

YOUNG QB GETS NOTICED

In the midst of this social whirl, there was also freshman football — and although Baugh remembers little about it, he was fast becoming the talk of the school.

"Hell, we only played a couple of games," he says, "and I can't even remember if we won any. I can't remember where we played, either — just that it was somewhere down on the (Trinity) river."

It was, in fact, LaGrave Field — an arena that over a period of decades became semi-legendary as a minor-

Dutch Meyer's first TCU squad in 1934 won 8 games and lost 4.

league ballpark, periodically hosting brilliant Double-A ballclubs and luminaries past and future ranging from Rogers Hornsby to Duke Snider.

But on a few occasions in the fall of 1933, it was the domain of a lanky kid from Sweetwater.

"There may not have been many (freshman) games that fall, but we saw enough," Pritchard says.

"Every time there was a game, we went down to La-Grave and watched Sam do some unbelievable things with a football."

The freshman games were played at the baseball park because recently constructed TCU Stadium was reserved for the varsity and old Clark Field was rather suspect, along with various other facilities.

"I remember the old basketball gym we had," Pritchard says, "which was distinctive mainly because it was very drafty. In those days, they flipped a coin before basketball games and if you won, you had your choice of goals.

"One time, our captain won the toss and told the referee, 'We'll take the wind.'"

Pritchard stayed at TCU for two years before transferring to the University of Texas to study law.

"It was a much bigger school," he says, "with about 10,000 to 12,000 students. I got a degree down there, but in my heart I have always remained loyal to TCU. It was

a place that I dearly loved.

"And one of the best things about it was Sam. He was our idol — our hero — but we were never in awe of him, because he was also our good friend. He got along with people very well — with everybody — and on the field he was a good leader.

"One thing a lot of people probably don't realize is that he was a very good student, very smart, and he used to spend a lot of time helping some of those guys on the team who were having trouble making their grades. I think he definitely helped some of them graduate.

"When Sam moved up to the varsity in 1934, we had a senior quarterback named Joe Coleman. He was a fine player and very well-liked and respected by everyone on campus, and he was also one of the team captains.

"But there was no doubt who the new quarterback was going to be."

TCU'S DATE WITH DESTINY

As the 1934 season approached, there was speculation about the crowd at quarterback (tailback in the single wing), but an article in the local paper noted that "Sam Baugh's passing may give him an edge."

Francis Schmidt had answered the call of destiny and

departed for Ohio State, where he was soon dubbed "Landslide Schmidt" for the merciless drubbings his teams administered — in his first two seasons, the Buckeyes outscored foes, 504-91 in 16 games — but became chiefly remembered for the 18-13 loss to Notre Dame in the famous 1935 game.

He was replaced by Dutch Meyer, who although he had coached the baseball and freshman football teams for several years, was still often referred to as "Leo" in the newspapers. By the time he concluded a 19-year career as head coach, it would become one of the most forgotten first names in history, and he would be universally known simply as "Dutch."

What was about to begin was one of the most amazing sagas in the history of college football — in which a small, practically bankrupt school far from the centers of media attention and elitist patronage would produce, in a few short years: three bowl champions, two super teams, and two national champions, one Heisman Trophy winner (Davey O'Brien), and two of the game's most legendary quarterbacks.

And forever after, it was acknowledged that L.R. (Dutch) Meyer was a top-rank innovator and a football coach of stunning ability.

"I guess you would have to say it was just flat unbelievable," says Don Looney, a favorite receiver of O'Brien's on the 1938 national championship team. "To think that a little ol' school like TCU would have two quarterbacks like Sam and Davey come along one right after the other defies logic.

"And those two guys did a lot more for TCU than just win a few football games.

"They brought the school a prestige it had never known before. And a fame that people still talk about today."

BAUGH SHOWS UNWAVERING CONFIDENCE

The era's opening salvo occurred in the unlikely venue of Brownwood, Tex. where the Horned Frogs opened

Jarrin' Jimmy Lawrence, an All-SWC halfback in 1933 and 1935.

the 1934 campaign against tiny Daniel Baker College.

A pattern that persisted throughout the season was established: Coleman started the game (and had significant playing time throughout), but Baugh was inserted whenever the Frogs wished to light the fuse.

But in the overall news scheme of the moment, the fact that TCU's sophomore quarterback had scored once and thrown three touchdown passes in a 33-7 victory was overshadowed by the fact that an intense manhunt had resulted in the capture of Bruno Richard Hauptmann, destined to be convicted and executed in the Lindbergh kidnapping case.

The next week, the Frogs defeated North Texas State, 27-0, before what was reported as being "the largest crowd ever to witness a TCU home opener" — 5,000 fans. By the end of the following season, TCU would be hastily adding seats to accommodate a crowd of nearly 40,000 for the SMU game.

In the Southwest Conference opener, the Frogs fell, 24-10, to Arkansas in a game that Julius (Judy) Truelson — a senior tackle in 1934 — remembers well.

"It wasn't one of Sam's better games," Truelson says, laughing, "but it also showed us something about the kind of player he was.

"We started Coleman at quarterback, and sometime late in the half we had built a 10-0 lead, and they put Sam in.

"The first thing he did was try to catch a punt on our one-yard line. He fumbled it, and Arkansas recovered and got an easy score to make it 10-7. Then early in the second half, we got backed up to about the five-yard line and Sam tried to throw, and they intercepted and ran it in to make it 14-10.

"Finally he got us backed up again deep in our territory and they intercepted another pass and went in to make it 21-10.

"So here he had cost us 21 points in pretty quick succession — and lost the game, as it turned out — but there was an interesting reaction. It never shook him at

all. He never lost confidence, and took us on a couple of drives late in the game, although we didn't score.

"It was a costly defeat, but I'm sure the coaches also saw something in him they liked that day. And I think that ability was part of what always made him such a good leader."

TCU TAKES CARE OF BAYLOR

From there, the Frogs whipped Tulsa and Texas A&M and rolled toward a crucial home game with Baylor in early November. On the day before the game a special train transported 1,200 Bear fans to Fort Worth, prompting the head of the local transportation board to put out a call for volunteers to help drive the visitors to the stadium for a pre-game barbecue. On Saturday, the Baylor band marched down Main Street on its way to the game.

Elsewhere, Babe Ruth was considering a $35,000 offer from the famed House of David barnstorming team, which was offering the concession that he would not be required to grow a beard like the other players.

And in St. Louis the brothers Dean — Dizzy and Paul — were asking owner Sam Breadon for a raise after earning a combined $11,500 for winning 53 games, including all four World Series victories, for the Cardinals in 1934.

Diz, in fact, confided to reporters that they had just made about $12,000 apiece on a barnstorming tour and weren't "worried about no wolves at the door this winter."

But in asking for a combined $40,000, for himself and his brother, Diz added that their recent success "ain't gonna make me unreasonable. Take some and leave some, I says, and Mr. Breadon will find us very reasonable and as I might say to him in a letter, hoping he is the same, I am yours truly, Dizzy."

By the end of the afternoon on Saturday, the Bears were also dizzy, having first been bombed by Baugh and then subjected to the indignity of watching him clinch a 34-12 win with a pair of fourth-quarter interceptions

from his safety position that led to two TCU scores.

But TCU's hopes of a SWC title died two weeks later when Bohn Hilliard led Texas to a 20-19 victory in a game in which the Longhorns passed for one yard and rushed for 320.

Baugh threw for 206 yards and two touchdowns, but the Frogs lost when fullback Taldon (Tillie) Manton, playing with an injury, missed two conversion attempts.

In what would within a week be termed a "dangerous, growing trend in the league," a Texas player slugged one of the officials after the game.

But just as the season reached its lowest ebb, the Frogs were presented with an intriguing opportunity: up next were the Rice Owls, an undefeated team so powerful they had attracted the attention of famed New York sportswriter Grantland Rice, who journeyed to Houston to watch them play TCU.

STRANGE HAPPENINGS, INDEED

Meanwhile, the news of the day stretched from the exotic to the wretched to the sublime.

The week of the Rice game, a page one headline in The Fort Worth Star-Telegram read: "Two Men Found Dead At Equator."

Actually, the two men were found on a waterless island in the Galapagos, having evidently died after their schooner hit a reef. They were identified by a passing ship's captain as a Norwegian and a Parisian, the latter being the rescuer of the former, who had recently been held prisoner by the Baroness Eloise Bonsquet de Wagner on a nearby island, of which she had proclaimed herself "Empress."

He was also "said to have been known by Vincent Astor and a member of the Roosevelt family."

Rather closer to home, the Arlington Downs racetrack outside of town was the scene of a murder involving a 97-pound, 17-year-old jockey who admitted killing the track's 80-year-old night watchman during a $5 robbery.

"I slept fine after I ran back to my bunk, because I didn't think you could kill him with one bullet like that," said the youth, who told police he needed the $5 to redeem a watch he had pawned to a stable boy. "I thought I just winged him.

"I heard about him being dead this morning and I didn't feel very good. I felt rotten and sick at the stomach, so I went back to sleep for awhile."

In the sports pages, negotiations with Breadon and general manager Branch Rickey had finally hit a snag or two, Dizzy Dean announced he had discovered a solution to the dilemma.

"Me and Paul may just buy the Cardinals and get this thing straightened out," said Diz. "We ought to have enough money pretty soon, and I wouldn't mind owning a ball club with a couple of pitchers like us."

The day of the game, a local headline proclaimed that "Everybody but TCU is expecting a Rice victory."

It was certainly understandable. The Owls' only blemish in nine games had been an early season tie with LSU. The following week they had beaten Purdue, 14-0, and had been rolling ever since. They were being considered for the Rose Bowl and had two running backs who had a shot at being all-Americans — Bill Wallace and John McCauley.

The Frogs were bruised and battered after the Texas game and even lost assistant coach Bear Wolf, who became ill on the eve of the game.

But on that day in Houston, TCU used a simple plan to near perfection. Forsaking their usual air game, they scored on an 80-yard opening drive — then used a withering defense led by Darrell Lester and Walter Roach to make it stand up in a stunning 7-2 upset victory.

Rough game, even for the refs.

Truelson remembers it like it happened last Thursday.

"When we took the ball on our first possession," he says, "Joe Coleman was at quarterback, and we just kept running Jimmy Lawrence at 'em until we were down on about their six-yard line.

"Then Joe called 32X — which was a reverse to Lawrence on which he was supposed to throw to Harold McClure. But he was covered, and Rice was swarming back there and it looked like Jimmy was trapped for a big

The day of the game, a local headline proclaimed that "Everybody but TCU is expecting a Rice victory."

loss when suddenly he threw back across the field to Coleman, who ran it in for the touchdown."

The TCU defense spent the remainder of the day cutting down Wallace and McCauley wherever they went, and generally frustrating the potent Owl attack.

Late in the game, however, the Frogs gave Rice a safety to obtain a free kick against the wind — and moments later the Owls were at the TCU nine-yard line, thanks to a 31-yard pass interference call.

Prominent among a crowd of hopping mad Frogs at the scene was Lawrence, who felt that the play had eluded the field judge, Dick Fisher.

Truelson, however, recalls that it afforded TCU's raging defense its finest moment.

"They were running out of the Notre Dame Box with an unbalanced line to the right," he says, "and on the first play they got down to about the five-yard line.

"On the next play, we threw 'em back for an eight-yard loss. On the play after that, they lost 15. On fourth down, they lost 15 more, and we took over out on about the 40. And that was pretty much the end of it."

Except for a post-game presentation by Lawrence, who — emulating his Texas counterpart of a week earlier — ran out onto the field and laid Fisher out.

"It was actually a little bit funny," Truelson says. "We were all out in the middle of the field celebrating, and Jimmy came running up and threw this big roundhouse right at Fisher, who was standing not far away.

"Except he missed him, and fell down. But he got up promptly and decked him with the left."

Mortified, Meyer rushed out, picked Fisher up off the ground, and said, "Oh, gosh — I just can't apologize too much for this. It's taken the kick out of the ball game for me, and I'm so sorry."

Good-naturedly, Fisher told Meyer to "forget about it — just a hot-headed boy, and I don't hold him any ill will."

He even went so far as to restrain some irate Rice fans trying to get at Lawrence, and to ask the media not to report the incident.

In 1935, the Horned Frogs posted a record of 12 wins and one loss, and were named national champions.

This finally resulted in an apology from Lawrence, who said, "I'm sorry, I just lost my head because I didn't think he should have called the play that way.

"Still don't."

There was soon newspaper commentary lamenting the decline of sportsmanship in collegiate athletics, but the Frogs were nevertheless ecstatic over their victory.

Particularly so since the offensive hero who had emerged in their finest moment was Joe Coleman — the selfless senior captain who had quietly played second fiddle to a more talented underclassman.

"Joe was a great guy and a very unselfish football player," Baugh says. "We always got along real well, and he tried to help me in any way he could. It made me feel good that he scored that touchdown against Rice."

Reflecting on the game in The Star-Telegram, Flem Hall decided that, "Rice's ambitions for the Rose Bowl or the Sugar Bowl got tossed into the soup bowl."

The following week, the Frogs showed up a tad flat, and were flattened, 19-0, by SMU.

A FITTING FINISH FOR THE FROGS

But there remained time in the season for one last grand gesture, and the Frogs were marvelously on cue.

Into TCU Stadium came a bona fide major college power of that day and time — the Santa Clara Broncos, coached by Maurice (Clipper) Smith.

They had lost once — to St. Mary's — but in battles against the two top teams on the coast they had whipped California and tied Rose Bowl-bound Stanford.

They also boasted probably the most colorfully named backfield in America — Salty Salatino, Frankie (Bomber) Sombrero, Friski Kaliski and Flash Falaschi.

But the Frogs won, 9-7, as Manton atoned for his misses against Texas by kicking the winning field goal late in the game.

"That was kind of a weird situation," Baugh says. "We played those guys three times when I was at TCU and may have beat 'em every time. And I think in two of those years they had the better team."

But Smith, recalling that after the Owl game Grantland Rice had called the Southwest Conference "the roughest and toughest in the country," paid tribute to TCU.

"Grantland Rice," he said, "was right."

And Rice, remembering Darrell Lester's play against the Owls, put the TCU lineman on his all-America team.

For the Frogs, the spotlight was beginning to warm up.

34

CHAPTER FOUR

Clash of the Titans

Memorable Fake Punt Links SMU, TCU Forever in 'Greatest SWC Game'

Although he was now a student at the great state university in Austin, Ed Pritchard returned to TCU at the tag end of November 1935. He returned to attend a football game that at the time was regarded as the most singularly momentous event in the 20-year history of the Southwest Conference.

Through the six decades that followed — until that conference eventually incinerated itself — it was remembered as the moment that indelibly stamped the SWC's presence on the national map; the moment that in certain measure paved the way for all the fame and glory, the legions of all-Americans, the national championships, the Heisman Trophy winners that followed, not to mention the almost immediate establishment of a major post-season game (the Cotton Bowl) in an SWC city.

It was also the gala social event of the year in Fort Worth, where it took on an aspect approaching that of a royal coronation.

It was in fact a collision of two unbeaten football teams, arch-rivals, whose particularly daring style of play had captured not only the attention — but the imagination — of the entire country. Or as one national report phrased it, "A showdown between two reckless aerial performers."

These were TCU and SMU, a pair of teams each sporting a 10-0 record and each led by an all-American back — Sam Baugh for the Horned Frogs and Bobby Wilson for the Mustangs. Linemen Darrell Lester of TCU, along with Truman Spain and J.C. Wetsel of SMU, were also all-Americans. The coaches were Dutch Meyer and Matty Bell, close friends and bitter rivals.

Awaiting the victor was the greatest prize in football at that time, pro or college: a trip to the Rose Bowl.

For weeks, both teams had been ranked among the top five in the country — the first time in history that the upstart SWC had been accorded such prestigious acclaim.

Once again, Grantland Rice was on hand to chronicle the further adventures of what was becoming his pet football league. But this time, he was joined by the cream of the sporting press from coast-to-coast. Hollywood luminaries poured into Fort Worth, spending extravagantly as if no one had ever heard of a depression.

Local publisher Amon G. Carter, friend of the late Will Rogers and tireless promoter of TCU, threw lavish parties for visiting dignitaries, and TCU Stadium's 28,000-seat capacity was hastily expanded.

It was estimated that by the kickoff, nearly 40,000 witnesses had jammed themselves into the stadium — including Pritchard.

"I didn't have a ticket, but I still had a lot of friends at TCU, and they got me into the game," he says. "So I was standing right there when Bobby Wilson caught that pass that beat us, 20-14.

"And it broke my heart."

In that feeling he was joined by an entire community, nurturing dashed hopes of a perfect season and a triumphant trip to California for the ultimate college football experience.

MERE WORDS CAN'T DESCRIBE...

But the long and short of it had only begun to be played out. By the time glowing accounts of the game had raced across the wires to their destinations coast-to-coast, every player on the field had been transformed into a Viking hero: a god of battle in a noble quest in which both victor and vanquished would live forever in Valhalla.

Typical was this account, in the memorably florid style

Tillie Manton (33) scrambles for extra yardage against SMU in 1935.

of the day, filed by Maxwell Stiles, sports editor of The Los Angeles Examiner:

"Streaking like a brown blur across the brown gridiron and arched in soaring flight against the blue background of bright Texas skies, a spiraling football sped on its meteoric way here this afternoon to give the wild Mustangs of Southern Methodist a 20 to 14 victory over Texas Christian.

"Thrown long and far and with unerring accuracy by Bob Finley, the right halfback of the Dallas team, the ball zoomed like a projectile down from its airway flight in-to the hands of Bobby Wilson, Southern Methodist's brilliant 147-pound candidate for a backfield berth on the 1935 all-America squad. Wilson caught the ball while he was in the grasp of a TCU tackler. He whirled like a dervish and spun over the goal line."

Topping Stiles only slightly in hyperbole was Bill Cunningham of The Boston Post, who wrote: "Maybe the garishly spangled hornsmen and drum thumpers of the Southern Methodist University band don't know the theme song of that sun-touched bourne of the squirtless grapefruit and the self-starting earth agues, else why in thunder didn't they parade out of this concrete dimple in the Western Plains banging *California, Here I Come* at the conclusion of their crusade against the local Christians here this throbbing afternoon?"

Cunningham went on to dub Wilson a "lizard-legged little bundle of mobile murder" but also declared that "brethren and beloved, Mr. Slingin' Samuel Baugh can chunk that cabbage."

The writer from The Kansas City Star called it a heroic battle that caught the national public fancy and made Fort Worth, for one afternoon, the football capital of the nation.

Significantly, most accounts from the leading observers of the day identified both teams as having been better than anything else the writer had seen that year. In the end, they wound up playing in the two most prestigious post-season games of that time — the Rose Bowl and the Sugar Bowl.

And while it was a glittering triumph for SMU and a bitter setback for the hosts, the losers may have achieved the greater fame in the long run. After the Mustangs had lost to Stanford in the Rose Bowl and the Frogs had defeated LSU in the Sugar, one ranking service declared TCU the national champion. And as the years rolled by, Baugh's fame far outstripped that of the other combatants.

But the real winner that November day in Fort Worth was a struggling league featuring a crowd of Texas teams (plus Arkansas) that suddenly came of age. From that moment on, any SWC team with the appropriate record was accorded a heretofore unknown respect — and before the 30's were gone, two of them (TCU and Texas A&M) had won national titles.

All of this was launched by the magical season of 1935, when the Frogs and Ponies enchanted the football world.

SIGNS OF THE TIMES

It was a season that began with great expectations at TCU, which managed to sell 2,200 books of advance season tickets, at a cost of $5.50 for five home games.

A total of 47 players reported for pre-season drills — somewhat less than the 90 who showed up at Texas, but there proved to be more quality on the TCU squad.

Among those who did not report was Paul Hill, a 250-pound tackle who had been counted on as a comforting presence in the line.

It was reported, however, that during the summer he had "found a position he does not wish to leave." This being the Depression era, he decided a job was more important than football — or college.

On September 8, Louisiana governor Huey Long was gunned down in the foyer of the capitol building in Baton Rouge by Dr. C.A. Weiss Jr., an eye, ear, nose and throat specialist who had clashed with him politically.

As thousands turned out to mourn The Kingfish, martial law was declared.

Amid such news of the day, there was still room in The Fort Worth Star-Telegram for a story headlined, "Miss Virginia Dunlap Gives a Slumber Party."

The paper also carried all the leading advertisements, including one for Carter's Little Pills urging the reader to "Wake up Your Liver Bile," and one that claimed BC Powder would relieve a headache in three minutes. A favorite, no doubt, was one that read, "If You Are Ruptured, Cut This Out."

An ad for Camel cigarettes assured the reader that "they are so mild you can smoke all you want," accompanied by the testimony of a young lady noting that "Famous athletes approve of them, so they must be mild, and when I'm tired I really get a lift from a Camel."

ROLLING RIGHT ALONG

The favorites in the SWC race were TCU, SMU and Rice — which had won the championship in '34 despite the upset by the Frogs, and still had its great running backs, Bill Wallace and John McCauley.

In addition to Wilson, SMU had a great all-around back in Harry Shuford, while TCU had the running of Jimmy Lawrence to balance Baugh's passing, along with Lester anchoring the line on both offense and defense.

In what amounted to a pre-season smoke screen, one report stated that Baugh was slated to share time with Vic Montgomery and Vernon Brown. Montgomery was indeed a prominent part of the attack for three years, but not as an "alternate" for Baugh.

As the season opener approached, interest in the team mounted, and 7,500 fans showed up at the stadium one

evening for Meyer's annual "ABC's of Football" seminar, in which the players were put through drills demonstrating various aspects of the game to the crowd.

On the opening weekend, a downtown theater featured *Top Hat*, starring Fred Astaire and "Fort Worth's own" Ginger Rogers, and 5,000 fans came out to watch TCU face Howard Payne, which was coming off an undefeated season. Scoring on a 10-yard run, Baugh crossed up the guests and launched a 41-0 rout.

Meanwhile, the co-favorites kept pace, as SMU buried North Texas State, 39-0, and Rice blanked St. Mary's, 38-0.

The next week, as a visiting Japanese admiral assured American officials that his "innate sense of sportsmanship" inclined him to side with Ethiopia in its struggle with Mussolini, Meyer took Friday off to scout upcoming foe Tulsa while deciding to start his second-string backfield against lightly regarded North Texas.

It nearly backfired, as the Eagles put up a stiff fight but eventually fell, 28-11. SMU, meanwhile, flattened tiny Austin College, 60-0, and Rice beat LSU in Baton Rouge, 10-7.

From there, the season progressed almost as predicted. The explosive finish provided by the Frogs and Mustangs has, historically, obscured the fact that until late November the SWC race was a tight three-cornered battle between the favored triumvirate.

In mid-October, SMU caught Rice with Wallace injured and shut down the Owls, 10-0, to win the first showdown among the top three teams. But from there, all three came thundering down the stretch in unblemished style.

In fact, until midseason it seemed the SWC had four teams vying for national recognition, as the Baylor Bears broke from the gate with six consecutive victories.

Baylor's amazing run of success lasted until TCU rolled into Waco on November 2 for a matchup of teams with identical 6-0 records. Playing in front of a highly vocal Homecoming crowd and boasting a pretty successful passing attack of their own, the Bears were hopeful of stopping TCU's seemingly invincible squadron.

But they never had a chance. Lawrence threw a touchdown pass, Baugh tossed three, and the defense — led by Lester and Wilson Groseclose — held the Bears to six first downs and 124 total yards while intercepting three

passes. The Frogs gained 340 yards — 204 in the air — and won, 28-0.

On the following Friday evening, the Frogs found themselves lost in a fog in New Orleans.

Fortunately, however, the Wolves of Loyola University made scant use of the fact that Baugh had difficulty throwing a wet ball through a hazy soup under dim lights. Lawrence scored twice and the defense conquered the fog and the Wolves, 14-0.

SMU, TCU STAKE THEIR CLAIMS

By that time, SMU was on its way to Los Angeles for a rare Monday engagement that would prove to be one of the most important games of the season.

There, in front of 50,000 awestruck witnesses, they dazzled the UCLA Bruins, 21-0, and writers on the West Coast began making plans to be in Fort Worth on November 30. From that point on, SMU — or possibly TCU, if the Frogs could defeat the Ponies — was the popular choice for the Rose Bowl.

"No doubt there will be an effort to secure Princeton for the Rose Bowl," one writer observed, "but you can have the Tigers. SMU has speed and more color than a block full of barber poles."

While the Mustangs, the toast of the coast, returned home to face Arkansas, the Frogs journeyed to Austin figuring to avenge the previous year's defeat by the Longhorns.

They were met at the train station by Texas coach Jack Chevigny, who graciously saw to their needs and then announced glumly that TCU would win the game — probably by a large margin. On Saturday, the Frogs turned him into a prophet.

In anticipation of rain, the Longhorns had tarped the field with their new $5,000 "raincoat," but the day broke warm and sunny — at least for TCU.

Baugh again threw for three touchdowns, and the Frogs ran a blocked punt in for a fourth, as Meyer sent his reserves into the game with five minutes left in the third quarter. The Longhorns made five first downs, had four passes intercepted, were outgained 355 yards to 79, and beaten, 28-0.

This brought Rice, at 8-1, into TCU Stadium, and

20,000 showed up to watch the battle. With Wallace and McCauley both healthy, the Owls were believed capable of returning the favor after being upset by TCU in 1934.

But George Kline took the opening kickoff and followed a wave of blockers 74 yards to the Rice 11, and on the first play from scrimmage Lawrence swept right, veered back to the left and darted into the end zone. With 20 seconds elapsed in the game, the Owls were on their way to a crushing 27-6 defeat.

The Owls actually acquitted themselves better than that — especially Wallace, who ran 20 times for 140 yards. But every time Rice seemed on the verge of battling its way back into the game, Baugh simply threw another touchdown pass. Again, he totaled three.

Getting into the spirit of the occasion, Flem Hall of The Star-Telegram came up with a marvelously purplish ode which began: "The flaming and furious Frogs of Texas Christian University, as audacious and clever a football battalion as ever stepped on a gridiron, put an end to all speculation to their prowess here on their own greensward Saturday afternoon by knocking the obstreperous Owls of Rice Institute into oblivion with a startling and smashing 27 to 6 score."

Further on, it was noted that the Christians' ascent to glory's peak had much to do with Slingin' Sam Baugh and Jarrin' Jimmy Lawrence.

STARS COME OUT TO WATCH

That set the stage for what might have been called the "Great Shootout," if anyone had thought of the term at the time.

"It was really something," Wilson says. "As far as it being a real head-knocking game, that it wasn't. But it was really and truly a great game for the spectators because it had a lot of scoring."

It justified the immense week-long buildup that had surfaced even during a timeout in the Princeton-Dartmouth game, when Steven Cullinam — center for the unbeaten and possibly Rose Bowl-bound Tigers — approached an official and said, "Know who the best team in the country is? Texas Christian."

Indeed, The Associated Press rankings the week of the game featured a three-way tie for first between Minnesota, Princeton and TCU. SMU was fourth, LSU fifth, Alabama sixth and Stanford, the eventual host team in the Rose Bowl, seventh. The Williamson Rating System had LSU first, followed by Minnesota, TCU and SMU.

As the week progressed, celebrities arrived — MGM casting director Rufus LeMaire, Columbia Pictures director Ralph Kohn with a party of six — and a Who's Who of coaching, led by Francis Schmidt of Ohio State, Bernie Bierman of Minnesota, Lynn (Pappy) Waldorf of Northwestern, Ray Morrison of Vanderbilt and D.X. Bible of Nebraska.

It was reported that Kohn's trip, with his guests, would cost him a minimum of $1,350, including $900 for plane fare and $175 a day hotel suites.

Luminaries attending the event eventually ranged from the president of Syracuse University to six Osage Indians who drove down from Oklahoma.

To accommodate the growing throng — tickets sold for $1.65 each — 3,500 seats were hastily added, bringing the stadium capacity to 31,000. By kickoff (2 p.m.), some of the estimated 40,000 who showed up had been there for six hours.

"By the time we arrived," Wilson says, "they were just driving up to the fence and climbing over. I don't know how they all made it inside.

"That was during the Depression, you know, and I think those people just wanted something to feel happy about. And this was it."

On Friday night, the Fort Worth Chamber of Commerce was host to visiting journalists at a dinner at The Worth Hotel. At game time, there were cars in the parking lot with plates from California, Pennsylvania, Florida and Michigan.

By the time Kern Tips and Cy Leland began a coast-to-coast radio broadcast originating on WBAP, the Frogs had been installed as slight favorites based on three factors: the home-field advantage, a slightly better showing against common opponents, and knee injuries that rendered SMU fullback Harry Shuford (twice all-SWC) and J.C. Wetsel unavailable for combat.

"Actually," Wilson recalls, "J.C. inserted himself into the game once, but he wasn't much use, 'cause he couldn't bend over."

No matter. After being led onto the field by their "midget horse," as The Star-Telegram reported, the Mus-

The 1935 TCU starting eleven who met SMU in the "Game of the Century."

tangs wasted little time marching 73 and 80 yards to build a 14-0 lead, with Wilson scoring the second touchdown.

After one aborted 74-yard drive, TCU scored on a short march late in the second quarter, closing it to 14-7.

At halftime, "Taps" was played, and, in the midst of the Depression, fans came up with $1,400 for a memorial for the recently deceased Will Rogers.

Baugh, whose receivers were having problems hanging onto his bullet-like deliveries, threw a touchdown pass to Lawrence early in the fourth quarter to tie the score. But Lawrence was injured on the play and left the game, setting the stage for a memorable finish.

THE PLAY OF THE DAY

Wilson and Finley, Shuford's replacement, drove SMU downfield again, until the Mustangs faced a fourth and four at the TCU 37.

SMU then lined up in punt formation, but Finley instead lofted a deep pass down the left sideline for Wilson, who caught it and went over the goal line with what

proved to be the winning score. TCU drove into SMU territory twice more, but failed to score.

When Wilson had scored earlier in the game, a slightly lubricated SMU fan had stood, addressing the neighboring witnesses, and declared that "the two greatest people in America are Bobby Wilson and President Roosevelt."

Later, when Wilson scored the winning touchdown, the man rose again and said, "Ladies and gentlemen, you may scratch President Roosevelt from the list."

For 60 years, the fake punt-pass remained one of the most famous plays in SWC history. And in the opinion of both Baugh and Wilson, a little over-hyped.

"I thought SMU deserved to win," Baugh says. "I'll give 'em this — they really set a good defense for us. They closed the gaps in the throwing lanes and basically took away the short pass, which was mainly what we relied on. We had to go to the medium pass, and the reason I was throwing the ball so hard is because they had closed gaps and I had to throw hard to keep it from being intercepted.

"But I threw it so hard the receivers couldn't catch it."

For the game, Baugh hit 17-of-44 for 180 yards with eight drops.

L.D. Meyer, however, scoffs at the notion that Baugh's passing cost TCU the game.

"He was throwing those balls right in there on the money," Meyer says, "and if you're a receiver, it's your job to catch those balls, no matter how hard they're thrown.

"I think the real problem was the pep talk Dutch gave us before the game. He normally didn't do a lot of that, but this time he was really trying to get us fired up, and he told us the winner would go to the Rose Bowl. We were mostly just a bunch of country boys, and this was the biggest thing that had ever happened in our lives.

"By the time we went out there, we are all tied up in knots, and Dutch always admitted that he thought he made a big mistake."

Baugh, however, says the biggest mistake TCU made was on the fake punt.

"The thing that galled us," he says, "is that they won on a play we were expecting; we just didn't stop it. It was reported as a daring gamble, but it was actually a routine play for that era.

"There was a rule back then that if you threw an incomplete pass into the end zone on fourth down, it was a touchback, and the ball came out to the 20. So if you were close enough, you might as well try it, 'cause you might score. And that's all they were doing."

Wilson says that afterward, he and Finley laughed about it.

"Everyone kept congratulating us on this great gamble," he says, "because they evidently didn't know the rule. So Bob and I agreed in the shower afterward that we wouldn't say anything about the rule. Finally, some guy doing research about 20 years later discovered it and wrote a story about it.

"We had planned to use the play on Lawrence because he came up so fast on coverage, but it turned out he wasn't in there when we called it. The two guys closest to me when I caught the ball were Baugh and the kid who replaced Lawrence (Harold McClure).

"I remember it as a pretty routine catch. All that whirling dervish stuff was a bunch of hooey.

"But as far as those dropped balls were concerned, I always thought they were catchable. Sam was throwing pretty hard, but he was right on target. With all due respect, I think Sam was the greatest passer we've ever had in the game.

"When I think about that game, the other thing I remember is that Matty sent me back into the game late, with instructions not to carry the ball because I was tired. But I ignored it and fumbled the ball at about their 18-yard line, and Sam brought 'em back to about our 35 before the clock ran out.

"That was a pretty impressive drive for that day and time, and I think if Sam had had a couple of minutes more, I would have been the goat instead of the hero."

TEAMS HEAD OUT WEST

Post-game accounts included a lengthy chronicle of prominent guests and their fashionable attire, such as, "Miss Eugenia White in a stunning green hat."

The following week, SMU finished a 12-0 season with a victory over Texas A&M and accepted the bid to the Rose Bowl. Banged up and strangely uninspired, the Mustangs failed to repeat their earlier dazzling display on the coast and lost, 7-0, to Stanford.

But the trip west earned the school enough money to pay off the mortgage on the SMU football stadium (Ownby) and inspired Dallas oilman J. Curtis Sanford to create a Texas-based post-season game. The first Cotton Bowl game — with TCU as the host — was played the following year.

TCU fans, meanwhile, were consoled by what turned out to be a much more enjoyable trip to the West Coast.

Sponsored by The Star-Telegram, a special train departed on the Tuesday following the SMU game — carrying the TCU players, staff and band, plus several hundred supporters, on a 4,202-mile round trip that would include sightseeing stops in Denver, Salt Lake City, San Francisco, Los Angeles and El Paso. In the midst of it all, on December 7, the Frogs would play Santa Clara in Kezar Stadium.

Highlights, as reviewed in the paper, would include breathtaking Colorado scenery, a ride through the seven-mile long Moffatt Tunnel, the Mormon Tabernacle, and Brigham Young's home — before the train rolled into San Francisco, where there would be two days and nights of trips to Chinatown ("The largest outside of China"), Golden Gate Park, Fisherman's Wharf, Telegraph Hill and the Twin Peaks.

On the day after the game, there would be "nearly 24

hours in Los Angeles, the attractions of which are too well-known to require enumeration."

For one person, an all-expenses paid, upper Pullman berth was available for $108.70. For those wishing to pay for their own meals and entertainment, the train fare and game ticket came to $56.05.

TCU won the game to finish the regular season at 11-1, and in the aftermath, West Coast commentators were once again agog over the exploits of a team from Texas.

The final score was only 10-6, but the Broncos had been saved from a worse fate only through a 77-yard return of a TCU fumble late in the game. The Frogs had a 206-127 edge in total yards, and Baugh had completed 14 passes — one to Lawrence for an early score — for 127 yards. Manton kicked a field goal for TCU's other points.

The ensuing Associated Press dispatch called TCU's performance "a thrill-a-minute display that once again demonstrated the superiority of Southwest football over the Pacific Coast variety, as the Horned Frogs passed their rivals dizzy."

FROGS SET SIGHTS ON THE BIG EASY

By this time, the Frogs had known for nearly a week that they would end the season in New Orleans — playing Southeastern Conference champion LSU in the Sugar Bowl. Two days before the Santa Clara game, Star-Telegram publisher Amon G. Carter received a telegram from James M. Thomson, his counterpart at The New Orleans Item-Tribune, advising him that 3,000 tickets for an otherwise sold-out game were being held for TCU fans.

"Fred Digby, our sports editor, tells me this will be the finest game ever played here," Thomson's telegram read, in part. "The Item and Tribune are anxious to extend to you and people coming with you every possible courtesy and render every possible assistance.

"While I have my opinion of probable results, and knowing that you wouldn't be happy if you didn't make a bet on your Texas team, I offer to bet you a box of Louisiana's finest oranges, which are the finest in the world, against a box of Texas grapefruit. Suggest you order the grapefruit now."

This, of course, necessitated another special train —

actually, three trains, since sales picked up briskly after the paper ran an ad promoting "The Great Feat of the Century," listing rates as low as $4 for a round-trip ticket (upper berth, Tourist Pullman). The coach rate was $11.26, but those really wishing to go in style could cough up $30 for a drawing room.

Eventually, more than 4,000 fans crammed themselves onto the trains, most of them garbed in the uniform of the day — a wide-brimmed white sombrero adorned with a purple Horned Frog. Well-wishers lined the platform, including one man in a business suit who kept saying over and over, "You lucky dogs."

TIME FOR SOME FUN, RELAXATION

By this time, the team had been in New Orleans for several days. Prior to that, however, local businessmen had gathered in the office of oilman Charles F. Roeser and presented the TCU coaches with "bonus" checks totaling $1,550.

"The whole thing was just amazing," says L.D. Meyer. "It was all orchestrated by Amon Carter, I'm sure. You can't imagine the extent to which he ran this town back then. He could do anything he wanted.

"He was a great supporter of TCU, and in a situation like that one, anything we needed we got. If we had to take a long road trip somewhere for a big game — poof — he got us a special train. He was a tireless supporter of anything he thought would promote Fort Worth."

TCU arrived in New Orleans with 23 players, four team members having opted to drive down themselves. Those four — Manton, Lawrence, George Kline and Melvin Diggs — showed up slightly late, but no one was especially upset.

"We made kind of holiday out of it," L.D. Meyer says. "Dutch had told us we were going down there for a whole week, and that we were going to enjoy ourselves. It was a big change from the way he was before the SMU game, but we sort of took the whole thing as a lark.

"Besides, it started raining a week before the game, and it was obvious that conditions were not going to be right for an exciting, high-scoring game.

"One day, Dutch gave me some time off so I could take his wife — my aunt — sightseeing around New Orleans. We went to a lot of different places and were having a big time when we finally got hungry. So we stopped in at this bar where you could stand up and they would bring you a plate lunch and something to drink.

"We got our food and I found us a table we could sit at, and my aunt had gotten one of these fancy, pink-looking drinks. She took a drink, and all of a sudden her eyes got real wide and she starting coughing and saying, 'Omigosh — that has alcohol in it! Dutch will kill me!'

"I don't know what she had thought it was, but I couldn't stop laughing."

STUCK IN THE MUD

Coached by Bernie Moore and boasting an array of stars that included Rock Reed, Abe Mickal, Jesse Fatherree and Gaynell Tinsley, the Tigers were 9-1 with only a narrow, early season loss to Rice. But although the two teams conducted a close, hard-fought battle, exciting it wasn't.

"Every time someone writes about that game, they usually say the field was a 'quagmire,' but that isn't the half of it," Meyer says. "There was standing water over your shoe-tops. After every play, when they put the ball down, an official had to stand there with his foot on it to keep it from floating away."

In the second quarter, TCU lost Lester, who broke his shoulder stopping an LSU drive at the goal line — the first of several Frogs, including Lawrence, who left the game with injuries. The Tigers eventually

Walter Roach, a 3-time All-SWC end in 1934-36.

got two points out of it when Baugh's foot touched the back line of the end zone while he was trying to pass.

But shortly after that, the Frogs drove to the LSU 19, where Manton kicked a 36-yard field goal that provided the decisive points in a 3-2 game.

"I'll never forget that," Meyer says, "because under those playing conditions, I was amazed that Tillie got the kick off. And from the time it left his foot, the whole way, it never rose more than two feet above the cross bar. We won that game on a line drive."

TCU stopped another LSU drive inside the 10 in the fourth quarter, then marched to the Tiger 23-yard line as the game ended. It was generally agreed that the key factor in the game was Baugh's punting, which kept the Tigers continually bottled up. He also broke loose and nearly scored on a 44-yard run in the final period.

Despite the weather, a capacity crowd of 35,000 viewed the game, and the Frogs took home a trophy and $25,000. Following the bowl results, the Williamson Rating Service declared TCU to be the top team in the nation.

Except for one pass on a fake punt play, it had been a glorious year for the Frogs. But that pass lingered in the memory far longer than all the purple prose used to describe it.

"Many years later," says L.D. Meyer, "when I was managing the Dallas (baseball) club in the Texas League, they hired Bob Finley as the caretaker for the ballpark.

"So I'd go in there every day, and when I saw him, I'd say, 'Hello, you S.O.B.'

"And he'd just laugh."

CHAPTER FIVE

Slingin' Sam's Senior Season

SWC Title Eludes Frogs Again, But Baugh Goes Out a Winner

On a pleasant November afternoon in 1936, TCU center Ki Aldrich broke the huddle, settled himself in his usual stance over the football, and slowly gazed up and down the line of scrimmage at the beleaguered Texas Longhorns.

"Gentlemen," he announced, "Mr. Sam Baugh is about to throw another pass. I don't know exactly where he's going to throw it, but I suggest you get yourselves ready, 'cause it's gonna be a good one."

Another moment of distress for the mighty men of the great state university — once again hopelessly outclassed by the troops of the small private school in Fort Worth. In the mid-1930's, it was a regular occurrence.

It was late in Sam Baugh's final season at that small but increasingly prominent school, and things had begun to fall into place.

Having lost Jimmy Lawrence, Darrell Lester, Taldon Manton, Wilson Groseclose and some other key players from the previous year's juggernaut, the 1936 team had started slowly. By midseason, the Frogs had lost twice and been tied once, and Baugh was limping around on a bad ankle. Prospects were not exactly cheery.

But as the Frogs approached what would become a mudbath in the Cotton Bowl — an intersectional game against Mississippi State — Dutch Meyer decided to rest his senior leader and hand a start to sophomore tailback Davey O'Brien. Although the game ended in a scoreless tie, the strategy was successful.

Thereafter, Baugh's ankle — and TCU — were much improved. And by the time the Longhorns got caught standing in the freeway, the Frogs were thundering down the stretch toward another glorious finish.

Historically, the season has always rested slightly to the rear of the famed 1935 campaign and the brilliant national championship year of 1938, in which O'Brien won the Heisman Trophy.

But for TCU, the 1936 season (9-2-2) was a fine affair in its own right. Once again, a stumble against old nemesis SMU cost the Frogs an SWC title, but they closed out Baugh's glittering career with decisive wins over two of the best teams in America — including a victory in the first Cotton Bowl game ever played.

And if 1935 was the year in which Baugh stamped his name in the national memory, 1936 was the year in which he convinced the shrewdest minds in the National Football League — including George Halas of the Bears and George Preston Marshall of the Redskins — that he was the quarterback of the future.

It was a season that began with Dutch Meyer holding court on the value of certain offensive styles, after he had helped coach a team of college all-stars to a 7-6 win over a team of pros coached by Halas.

"Passes did the trick," he said. "And you know, I can't help but feel that if we'd stuck to them a little more, we would have won by a wider margin.

"The game certainly proves a long-contended point: the Southwest Conference — and Southern — players are in a class by themselves at the aerial game.

"The pros are big, clever and tough. But there's no amount of brawn that pass trickery can't overcome."

Noting that some of the team's key players — including Lawrence — had played for him at TCU, he added, "It just naturally makes a difference when you know every player like he was your son."

With the season approaching, Meyer was asked if his remarks meant that Baugh would be throwing even more than in the past.

"Oh, maybe so, maybe not," he said, coyly. "But one thing's for sure — the Southwest will certainly get a lot

of good advertising out of that game.

"It may lead to our style taking over all over the country."

YEAR-LONG CELEBRATION

On September 10th, TCU opened its pre-season drills while the newspapers reported that President Roosevelt — running for re-election against Alf Landon — had stood in the rain and told a cheering crowd in South Carolina that the Depression was over.

"America," he said, "has turned a corner."

So had the Arkansas football team, evidently. There were disturbing reports out of Fayetteville that the players had all shaved their heads except for one row of bristles standing erect on top — so that they would look like, well, Razorbacks.

There were editorial suggestions that this might be an unhealthy trend.

This year, Dutch's "ABC's of Football" demonstration drew a smaller crowd — about 4,000 — but an added bonus was an impromptu performance from the TCU band.

It was also the year of Texas' Centennial — the 100th anniversary of the heroic defense of the Alamo and General Sam Houston's victory at San Jacinto over the Mexican general, Santa Anna.

It prompted a year-long, statewide celebration. And in honor of the occasion, Fort Worth built a coliseum and named it after Will Rogers — whose widow attended the opening ceremonies as a guest of Amon Carter.

A civil war had begun in Spain, and in Beaumont a one-eyed circus elephant named Trilby was reported to be crying and in "deep remorse" after killing a trainer who startled her.

Mutt and Jeff, Blondie, Dick Tracy, Popeye, Oh Henry and Tillie the Toiler were popular cartoon fare in the newspapers, where ads for Camel cigarettes were becoming more elaborate:

"Touchdowns like that send chills up and down my spine," a young woman exclaimed in one, after watching a long run. "I get so worked up after a game I can't enjoy my food."

Fortunately, "famous sports announcer" Ted Husing

was on hand with helpful advice: "You should smoke Camels between courses and after eating. Camels help ease the strain for me and give me a feeling of digestive well-being."

Downtown theaters featured *The Gorgeous Hussy*, starring Joan Crawford, Robert Taylor, Lionel Barrymore, Franchot Tone, Melvyn Douglas and Jimmy Stewart, along with Gene Autrey and the Lightcrust Doughboys in *Oh, Susanna*.

Gulf announced the introduction of its new "autumn gas" — developed especially for football fans.

And in Brownwood, TCU barely scraped by Howard Payne, 6-0, in the mud. Baugh engineered a 98-yard drive culminating in a scoring pass with less than a minute left in the game to save the Frogs from total embarrassment.

The next week in Lubbock, it got worse as Texas Tech rushed Baugh well enough to escape with a 7-0 upset win, in front of a record crowd of 13,000 who happily ignored a howling wind and soggy game conditions.

With Arkansas' freshly shaved Razorbacks and their renowned quarterback, Jack Robbins, coming to town, Meyer was in a dour mood. The daily dispatches from the practice field revealed that Dutch was "irritable" and workouts were getting longer.

In two games, TCU's vaunted offense had produced six points, the ground attack was absent, and the line could not protect Baugh from the rush. Finally, at midweek, Meyer announced an impending shake-up: he was thinking of starting O'Brien at tailback (quarterback) and moving Baugh to right halfback. When the team lined up that way in practice, the offense seemed to click.

When Arkansas arrived on Friday, Baugh and Robbins posed together while the papers reported that the Razorbacks would be favored to win.

Later, Meyer would say that if TCU had received the kickoff, it had been his intention to play O'Brien at tailback for at least a quarter before inserting Baugh. But since the Frogs kicked off, he decided he needed Baugh at safety.

Or perhaps he changed his mind when the towering senior approached him before the game and said, "Just put me in there at quarterback, and I'll play you a game of football."

It was no idle boast, as he turned in one of the best games of his career, and O'Brien was never needed.

HARD-FOUGHT CONTESTS

Still, it was a tense battle much of the way, and Meyer spent most of it squatting on the sideline, tearing up clumps of grass at an alarming rate and growling, "plunk-mutter" to himself. Occasionally, this was alternated with, "mutter-plunk."

Finally, even trusted assistant Mike Brumbelow decided to leave him alone.

An early surprise for the Hogs was the emergence of a TCU ground game, with Glenn (Donkey) Roberts barreling through wide gaps at six yards per pop.

In desperation, Robbins threw 41 times, but it wasn't enough. Baugh threw for 183 yards and dropped a 40-yard punt dead inside the Arkansas five to set up the clinching score — a pass to Vic Montgomery — in the final period. Arkansas scored with two minutes left to close to 18-14, but never got the ball back.

It would turn out to be Arkansas' only conference defeat, but for the moment it was simply a great mood-lifter for Meyer — who rushed into the shower after the game and lifted Baugh, naked, off the floor with a congratulatory bear hug.

But overall, Baugh did not come out in good shape. He sustained shoulder and ankle injuries, and during the week before the Tulsa game he caught a cold.

All of which convinced Meyer to go with his second-string backfield — not in contempt of the Golden Hurricanes but in the conviction that a loss there would be preferable to one the following week in College Station.

But with three minutes left in the half and TCU trailing, 7-0, Baugh and Meyer lost their patience more or less simultaneously, and in came Slingin' Sam to rally the troops.

He threw for 180 yards and put the Hurricanes in a hole that led to the winning points with a punt out of bounds at the Tulsa one-yard line. Montgomery threw a touchdown pass, and Walter Roach kicked a last-minute field goal for a 10-7 win.

But Baugh's physical condition did not improve, and the next week he went to Meyer with another suggestion — this time, that he put O'Brien in. Former Crowell High School star Dick Todd was beginning to roll for the

Aggies, and prudence seemed to outweigh bravado.

An alliterative headline in The Star-Telegram could have been taken as a warning: "Can Crowell Crusher Crash Christians' Citadel?"

Maybe they also should have printed the answer: "Certainly."

"We hadn't lost to A&M in 12 years (there had been two ties), and I just about begged Dutch to go with Davey this time," Baugh says. "I told him I really thought Davey was ready, and I just couldn't go. Hell, I was limping around like a cripple, and Davey was getting better every week.

"What I was really worried about was me being back there at safety on defense, 'cause when Todd got turned upfield, he wasn't one to wait on you.

"Well, Dutch wouldn't do it. He said he needed me in there. So Todd makes two long touchdown runs that beat us, and he was so far ahead of me I couldn't have hit him with a handful of gravel."

FROGS SURVIVE MONSOON

At this juncture in the season, "Texas-Mississippi Week" arrived as part of the centennial festivities, accompanied by a monsoon that would have raised eyebrows in Bombay.

One local high school game between arch-rivals Paschal and Poly was actually canceled. But on Friday night, the rain eased enough to allow the North Side Steers to sludge to an 18-0 victory over the top high school team in Mississippi, the Kossiusko Whippets.

On Saturday, the Frogs and Orange Bowl-bound Mississippi State weren't so fortunate. The rain resumed, and the two teams met in the mud at the Cotton Bowl before 3,500 lucky fans, almost none of whom drowned.

On game day, the papers had carried photos of Bulldog quarterback Charles (Pee Wee) Armstrong, usually with the caption: "He's Maroons' Sammy Baugh."

But neither was much in evidence during the game. Meyer, in fact, had decided the moment had arrived to take Baugh's advice and rest him for a week. In addition to his other maladies, Baugh had injured his throwing hand in the A&M game. When asked what was wrong with it, he simply said, "Stove up."

In 1936, Baugh & Co. put together a 9-2-2 record and played in the first Cotton Bowl.

The starting assignment went to O'Brien, referred to in one pre-game account as "the Irish infant," and Armstrong had enough on his hands just catching the center snaps, never mind throwing them to someone else.

In a game that produced 120 total yards, four first downs and 44 punts, the highlight was a 60-yard punt by O'Brien late in the game that got the Frogs out of a hole and ensured that the battle would indeed end at 0-0.

But Meyer's strategy had paid off. When Baylor rolled into TCU Stadium on Halloween, the grinning Jack O' Lantern awaiting them was a rejuvenated Sam Baugh. And for TCU, a second season was about to begin.

TURNING THE CORNER

The Bears came equipped with their own celebrity — Lloyd Russell, "The Crooning Quarterback."

Russell's claim to fame had begun two years earlier, when he had suddenly burst into song while running a punt

back for a touchdown. While it was agreed that he was no Bing Crosby, he became a favorite of fans and media.

Russell, a genuinely skilled tailback, attributed it to a reflex he could not explain.

"I have a peculiar habit of singing after the ball is snapped, often when I'm tackled," he said. "Some of the opposing players have told me that just before I am tackled I start mumbling and singing. I don't willfully start singing, but I have caught myself doing it."

Grateful for the publicity, Baylor coach Morley Jennings graciously offered an alternative scientific view: "Tommyrot."

At any rate, the game was billed as a duel between the two quarterbacks — one that never materialized.

Feeling fit once again, Baugh threw for three touchdowns in the first 20 minutes and took the rest of the day off. Eventually, the Frogs won, 28-0.

Next came Texas, a team whose fortunes and head coach were fading fast.

In answer to an early week query about defensing Baugh, Longhorn coach Jack Chevigny said, simply, "The only way Baugh can be stopped is if he stops himself."

At midweek, in fact, the report arrived from Austin that the Longhorns had stopped working on defense, regarding it as "hopeless" and a waste of time.

"Our only hope," Chevigny said, "is to try and outscore them."

In this, the Longhorns were never close. The Frogs led by 20 at halftime, eventually rolling up 24 first downs and 316 yards in a 27-6 rout. Harold McClure scored four times, and Baugh — who had been held out of drills all week — hit 14 of 19 passes and contributed a 61-yard interception return.

After the Texas team returned to Austin, Chevigny announced that he would resign at the end of the season.

Next up were the Gents of Centenary, in a game distinguished only by the fact that it was the last one Baugh ever played at Amon Carter Stadium.

And he played very little — throwing two touchdown passes in the first quarter and then turning it over to O'Brien, who threw two more in a 26-0 victory.

Given that it was the final home game of a player who had in effect changed the history of the university, the immediate clamor for Baugh after Meyer took him out is understandable. By the end of the game, Dutch was not a popular man.

Editorialists rushed to defend the coach's reasoning — saving his recently wounded star for the three grueling road games (Rice, SMU, Santa Clara) left on the schedule. One, however, did suggest that it might have been fun to leave Baugh in a game like that, "just to see how many passes he could complete."

But if Meyer was catching a little fan flak, he could at least take solace in the fact that the U.S. Army had not marched in and ordered him off the job.

It happened that week to Oklahoma coach Biff Jones, who happened to hold a commission as a major and was still on active duty, although he had been coaching for the past 10 years.

It was the latest in a series of mishaps for Jones — once a famous coach at West Point — who had left LSU two years previously after a run-in with Huey Long. Now, he was informed by the War Department that he had been reassigned to Fort Leavenworth.

Elsewhere that week, the forces of General Francisco Franco fought their way into Madrid, and David Brooks, the nephew of Lady Astor, fell to his death from the window of a 14th-floor Park Avenue apartment. The death was ruled an accident.

Locally, Sheriff A.B. Carter pinned a deputy's badge on Baugh, possibly feeling that this might help him gun down the Rice Owls when the Frogs opened their final three-game road swing in Houston.

More useful, however, was a fourth-quarter interception by Aldrich that stopped a Rice drive and turned the tide of a tough battle, which TCU eventually won, 13-0.

Baugh completed 16 passes for 153 yards and a touchdown, and the Frogs had a 319-143 edge in total yards. But when the Owls swept downfield midway through the fourth quarter, they trailed by only six points.

Aldrich halted the drive with a pickoff at the TCU 25, returning it five yards. From there, the Frogs launched a 70-yard clinching drive with a seldom used trick play, in which Donkey Roberts moved upfield on a trap, then pitched back to Baugh when the Owls closed in.

The play worked for 23 yards and led to a clinching touchdown moments later by Scott McCall.

This left the Frogs (4-1) tied with Arkansas for the league lead and needing only a win over arch-foe SMU to claim at least a share of the title that had thus far eluded them during Baugh's career.

THE DUTCH AND MATTY SHOW

It also set the stage for another annual installment of the long-running soap opera co-starring Dutch Meyer and Matty Bell, in which the coach of the underdog team wept profusely throughout the week, prayed to God for remission of all sins, and expressed the hope that his poor, outmanned troops could just have life and limb spared, since they were necessary for the support of their mamas.

Typically, this concluded with a game-day locker room speech in which the coach, apparently near death, finally blubbered that he could happily meet his maker if he could take with him just one last win over Dutch/Matty.

For 15 years, this routine made the TCU-SMU game the bane of professional bookmakers.

This time it was Matty's turn, and the Frogs had scarcely finished toweling off in Houston when he announced that the Mustangs had no chance.

"How can you expect a team like ours (4-4 with a three-game losing streak) to beat TCU, the way they're going, and with Sammy Baugh hot as a firecracker?" he said. "Yeah, we know what he's going to do, but that doesn't mean we can stop it."

Ominously, the Frogs lost Scott McCall early in the week when his "trick knee" became swollen as a result of a hit in the Rice game. By Saturday, it hardly mattered.

Making their second trip to Dallas during the 1936 season, the Frogs received their second mudbath. Torrential rains had turned Ownby Stadium into a morass, and the game into a wash.

It became, in fact, a historical footnote to Baugh's career — the first game he ever played in which he failed to complete a pass. He threw five, and SMU intercepted two of them.

TCU had 161 yards to 60 for SMU, but the score duplicated the Mississippi State game, 0-0.

Late in the first quarter, McClure bolted 53 yards toward what would have been the game-winning score — but he was dragged down at the SMU seven. From there, TCU made four yards, and Meyer's field-goal attempt — as described in the game account — "sailed a few yards to the East of the goal post."

SMU mounted a brief threat following a fumble recovery in the second half, but Walter Roach blocked a field-goal attempt. Thereafter, the teams simply sloshed to a dreary finish.

A disappointed witness to Baugh's final SWC game

> *"Sam was a big celebrity — they really loved him out there. They all thought he was the greatest quarterback in the world."*
>
> —L.D. Meyer

Baugh greets TCU fans at the train station upon the team's return from the Santa Clara game in 1936.

was Francis Schmidt, the man who had officially presided over his arrival, although he had never coached him.

"It was more than a shame that it rained today," said Schmidt. "It was a tragedy."

The following week, Arkansas scraped by Texas, 6-0, and the SWC crown once again eluded TCU.

TOASTS OF THE TOWN

And for the third straight year, there was Santa Clara at the end of the schedule, offering redemption for the Frogs.

As usual, a special train was organized by The Star-Telegram. Rates were rising, however, ranging this time from $75.53 to $135.30.

The attraction, however, was even greater — the Broncos, now coached by Buck Shaw, were the only remaining unbeaten, untied team among the nation's major colleges. They had given up only 13 points in seven games and numbered Stanford (13-0) and Auburn (12-0) among their conquests. The Frogs, with McClure out and others injured, were heavy underdogs.

In less than a month, the Broncos would roll into the Sugar Bowl and whip LSU, 21-14, in a game that was nowhere near that close. But for the third straight year, they were unable to handle the Frogs.

With 40,000 on hand in Kezar Stadium, TCU won, 9-0, handing the Broncs the only defeat they would suffer through the 1936 and '37 seasons. Once again, the key was pitching and defense.

Early in the game, Nello (Flash) Falaschi returned an interception to the TCU three-yard line, but the Broncs were stopped cold, and later missed a field-goal attempt.

From there, Baugh took over, completing 13 of 26 passes for 122 yards and a touchdown, and TCU added a field goal to clinch it, as Baugh's punts kept Santa Clara pinned down. Afterward, the usual superlatives from the West Coast writers popped up:

"They couldn't stop 'Slingin' Sammy Baugh.'"

"He put wings on the football."

"Baugh did it almost single-handedly."

While it was debated whether or not TCU would indeed meet once-beaten Marquette in the inaugural Cotton Bowl, the Frogs stayed in San Francisco and celebrated.

"Amon Carter had arranged that special train for us again," L.D. Meyer recalls, "and for all anybody knew, this was going to be our last game together, so they were prepared to go all out for us.

"Dutch said we were gonna stay a week, break training, whatever. We had just knocked off the only unbeaten team in the country, and everyone was feelin' good. The town was ours.

"Sam was a big celebrity — they really loved him out there. They all thought he was the greatest quarterback in the world."

So, for several nights, the boys were on the prowl.

"One night, we were sitting in this bar — me, Sam and Willie Walls — and this guy comes up and starts talking to us. And he says, 'You guys see that football game with TCU? Boy that Sam Baugh has got to be the greatest passer in history.'

"So Willie says, 'Ah, he ain't that good — I've seen better.' And the guy gets really mad and starts talking real loud, telling us we don't know anything about football and that there's never been anyone greater than Sam.

"So finally, we said, 'You want to meet him?'

"He looks at us and he says, you know Sam Baugh? So we pointed to Sam across the table and said, 'You been talking to him for 30 minutes.'

"Well, the guy starts lookin' at Sam, and pretty soon he's squinting, and checking him out, and suddenly he runs out the door and comes back in with a newspaper — and there's Sam's picture. He couldn't believe it.

"So after that, he insisted on taking us around and showing us the town. We went all over San Francisco, club after club, watched all these great floor shows, and everywhere we went he would stop the music and announce that the great Sam Baugh was with us. And he told us, 'Nobody pays but me.'

"We called him Good Time Charlie, but he finally drank so much he just kinda fell over in his seat when we were in a cab, so we had the cabbie take him home."

COTTON BOWL-BOUND

There had been much speculation that TCU — worn and wounded after another grueling, 12-game campaign

Baugh and Marquette quarterback Buzz Buivid admire the Cotton Bowl trophy, which TCU won, 16-6, in 1937.

— would decline the honor of playing in the first-ever Cotton Bowl game. For one thing, the team's two previous trips to Dallas that year had resulted in muddy, scoreless ties — the last of which had cost them a championship they thought they could have won on a dry field.

Alternate speculation suggested that since the Frogs were so popular in California, Dutch might be tapped to coach in the more prestigious East-West game, and take his star players with him. And Marquette, which had rolled through unbeaten before losing its final game to Duquesne, was reportedly growing cool on the idea of playing in the new bowl.

Additionally, there was now annual agitation at the December NCAA meetings in New York, where dark fears of professionalism in college athletics were voiced, the decline of sportsmanship and a disregard for tradi-

tion were decried, and anguished complaints about the quest for the almighty dollar were heard.

Academics regularly rose on the convention floor to wonder what all this had to do with higher education — and where it was leading — and each year there was a new movement to boycott the bowls. This was customarily led by schools that would never have been invited to one in the first place.

But when the smoke finally cleared, Marquette coach Frank Murray had agreed to bring his "Golden Avalanche" to Dallas to face the Horned Frogs — and the stage was set for one last great "duel" in Sam Baugh's college career.

The distinguished alter-ego in this one was Marquette's Ray (Buzz) Buivid, who had been placed on several all-America teams and was as famed for his passing in the Midwest as Baugh was in Texas. Although Larry Kelley of Yale had just won the second Heisman Trophy ever presented, with Nebraska's Sam Francis second in the voting, Buivid had finished third and Baugh fourth.

Murray proved to be an entertaining subject for local writers, as was halfback Art Guepe — the future coach — whose "popoff" personality was markedly different from that of his taciturn twin brother, Al.

"I've never seen your boy, Baugh," said Murray one day, talking to the writers while watching his team practice, "but I believe Buivid can throw with any of them. From what I hear, Buivid is probably better than Baugh on long passes, and you can't beat that boy for accuracy. Why — Hey, nice pass, Buzz! — why, that boy is uncanny for accuracy. It's just a little warm for us right now, but I think the temperature will drop by game time, and we'll show you something."

As the game — and threatening weather — approached, Dutch Meyer devoted himself to muttering about "trickery" in the Marquette offense, which he feared would be unfathomable to his poor defense.

The TCU scrubs, running the Marquette offense, had a field day in practice. But this became a weekly occur-

TCU piles up the Marquette offense in the inaugural Cotton Bowl on New Year's Day 1937.

rence during Meyer's career, and was eventually suspected of being staged so that Dutch could cry to the press about the hopelessness of his team's situation.

The Frogs were truly banged up, and it was soon announced that Vic Montgomery would have to replace the injured McClure at halfback and "Little Dutch" Meyer would have to replace Walls at end, since he had cracked a bone in his foot.

For TCU, it proved to be a historic injury. L.D. Meyer had certainly played well enough during his career to earn his nickname — "Tiger" — but it had always been obvious that baseball was his future. But in the last game they ever played for TCU, he and Baugh hooked up in a memorable performance.

AN ENCORE FOR NO. 45

For the inaugural installment of J. Curtis Sanford's great dream, TCU wound up making $10,000 as the winning team and Marquette was paid $6,000. At the kickoff, there were 17,000 witnesses in the stands — who were treated to better weather than they had expected and a game quickly taken over by the Horned Frogs.

At halftime, TCU held a 16-6 lead, and "Little Dutch" — with two touchdown catches, an extra-point kick and a field goal — had scored all the Frogs' points.

By that time, his uncle had begun emptying the bench — every player on the TCU sideline (27) saw considerable action — and the Golden Avalanche, despite decent games from Buivid, Guepe and future NFL star Ward Cuff, could never close the gap.

"The first half was pretty interesting" Meyer says. "Marquette had a good team, and when they came out they were pretty spizzed up, and that guy Guepe was talking to everyone."

Guepe, who among other things returned punts for Marquette, was even talking to Dutch Meyer.

"I was kicking the ball away from him, which was what I normally did," Baugh recalls, laughing, "and he was gettin' pretty frustrated.

"So one time after I kicked one out of bounds, he swerves over to our sideline and runs past Dutch and hollers, 'Hey Dutch — tell Sam to kick me one!'

"So the next time we kicked, I decided, what the hell, and punted it right to him. Danged if that little sucker didn't run it all the way back (60 yards) for a touchdown!"

But it was Marquette's only score, and until Dutch started flooding the field with reserves, the guests had little success stopping the Frogs, who finished with a 318-189 edge in total yards. Used very little in the second half, Baugh threw for 100 yards in his final game.

"They were real scrappy," Meyer says, "but I just don't think they had ever seen a passing attack like the one we had.

"I had a good day, but actually the whole offense did. One of the catches I made was a legitimate touchdown pass (55 yards), but the other was one where Sam threw it to Montgomery and it bounced off Vic and I happened to be standing there and I just caught it and ran it in."

As the day wore on, TCU's 12 graduating seniors spent more and more time on the bench. Finally, late in the fourth quarter, Dutch responded to a growing clamor in the stands and put Baugh back into the game, one last time.

As the famous No. 45 trotted back onto the field and reported to the official, thousands of TCU fans rose with a tremendous cheer, and said goodbye.

Thus ended what up to that point had been the most illustrious career in the history of Texas football.

Baugh and his fiancee, Edmonia Smith, visit with the press after TCU's Cotton Bowl victory.

CHAPTER SIX

Sam Baugh's Brush with Baseball

In the course of a lifelong experience that often placed him on the same playing surface with individuals now in the Hall of Fame, L.D. Meyer had the opportunity to observe many men who seemed born to play professional baseball.

One of them was Sam Baugh.

"He was definitely a big-league third baseman," says Little Dutch, who spent a total of six seasons in the major leagues with the Cubs, Tigers and Indians. "He had the greatest arm I ever saw, and tremendous hands. He could catch anything — and then fire those strikes to first base from behind his ear all day long.

"I played for several years in both the majors and minors and then coached and managed for many years after that — largely in the Texas League. In all that time, I don't remember seeing anyone better than Sam at going behind the bag for a ball, and then throwing the guy out at first.

"He had good range, and with those hands he could grab anything. And that long throw — which was a problem for so many guys — was a piece of cake for him.

"Of course, I wouldn't want to be the one to say he couldn't hit a curve ball . ..."

This one brings a hearty cackle from Baugh, who says, "Actually, I think it was the changeup — I never could wait on it."

In any case, it was Meyer, a slick-fielding second baseman, who made it to the majors. He compiled a .264 lifetime average and was sometimes a regular — but spent most of his career battling for a starting role against the likes of Billy Herman, Charlie Gehringer and Joe Gordon.

A somewhat lengthier list of his teammates would include Rudy York, Pinky Higgins, Hank Greenberg,

Birdie Tebbetts, Bobo Newsome, Schoolboy Rowe, Tommy Bridges, Hal Newhouser, Virgil Trucks, Dizzy Trout, Lou Boudreau, Bob Lemon, Bob Feller and Allie Reynolds.

"I think Sam could have played in the majors if he'd put his mind to it — but he was such a good athlete I think he could have done anything he put his mind to," Meyer says. "And of course, when Dutch first recruited him, he didn't know anything about his ability to play football.

"That was some deal. The (TCU) athletic department back then had two cars they could use for road trips — a Cadillac and a jump seat Chevrolet — and you could get about 12 guys into them.

"So every year, Dutch would pick 12 guys off the team and they would barnstorm for awhile, warming up for the season. They went to different places, and it was just by chance that they wound up in Sweetwater that year when Sam was playing on the town team."

TAKING RISKS EARLY

Chance, during the Depression, was usually a major factor in the success or failure of any career or business venture — and along with Hollywood, professional baseball stood as one of the brightest beacons on a dark horizon. When so many were broke, the idea of making money — good money — playing a kid's game was an irresistible lure for thousands of men and boys.

And since so many students were being educated on credit, no one was particularly fussy about summer employment. So, during the off-season, the boys would often go touring on their own.

"Every summer," Meyer says, "we would go down to Refugio and play baseball. We would ride the bus down there — me, Sam, and Jimmy Jacks.

"They had struck oil down there, and it seemed like they were all millionaires. It was a very rich town, and

Baugh signed with the St. Louis Cardinals in 1938 and advanced to their Double-A team in Columbus.

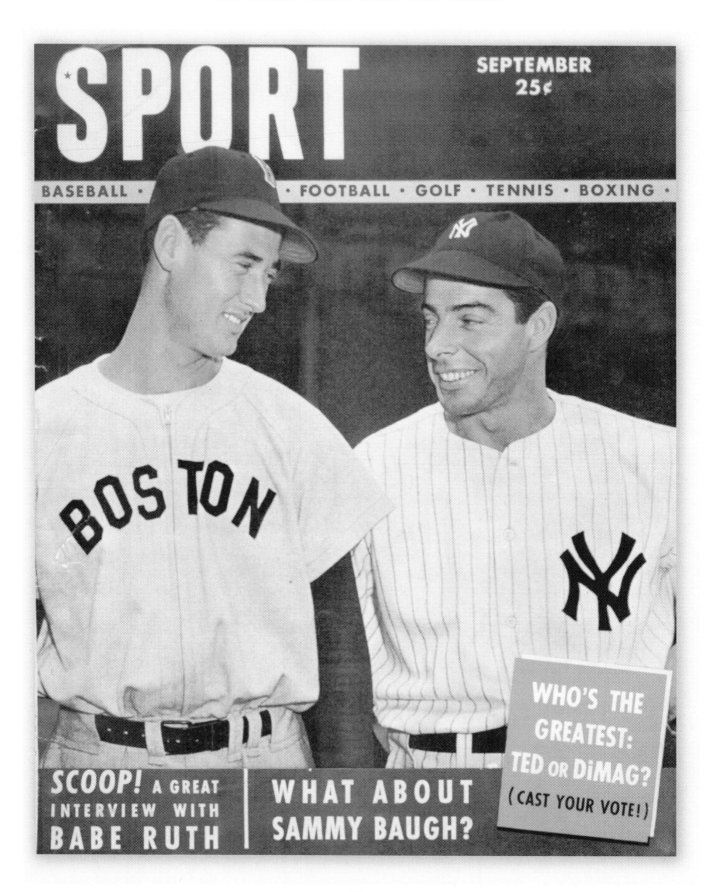

everyone in it had money.

"They had built a fine ballpark with a beautiful grandstand, and a bunch of guys would come in in the summer and play ball, and they treated all of us just great.

"They had big crowds at the games, and they loved ballplayers. You couldn't buy a lunch in that place. And if you hit a home run, you could walk around the stands holding your cap out and they would stick $5 bills in it.

"When we weren't playing ball we worked as swampers on a truck sometimes, but it was a great life. When we first went down there, we got off the bus and they told us to go over to the Riles Drug Store and check in. The owner of the store was the manager of the baseball team.

"You'd go over there and check in, and they would sign you up for $185 a month, plus room and board."

There was also the opportunity for romance, although Meyer recalls that Jacks, throwing caution to the winds, wound up with a little more than he bargained for.

"The first day we were there," he says, "we spotted these three real pretty girls sitting in a parked car, and we figured we ought to get to know them. So we had a coin flip to see who would go over and strike up a conversation. Jacks won the flip and eventually wound up married to one of them."

With the air of a man who has escaped certain doom, Meyer says, "Y'know, I used to think about that a lot. What if I had won that flip?"

USED TO BE CALLED 'FUN' BACK THEN

For one and all, however, it was a profitable summer, at a time when keen-eyed scrutiny by governing bodies had not progressed to its current levels.

Don Looney recalls working one summer in the oil fields and coming back with enough cash to purchase more than his normal share of season tickets — with which he then turned a $4,000 profit and bought a new car.

Once, during Baugh's career at TCU, there was a light-hearted item in the paper noting that the victory over LSU in the Sugar Bowl had cost the star quarterback $3 — which he had bet on the Tigers.

In current circumstances, this report would be the occasion of Death By Swivel Chair in high administrative offices, but 60 years ago it was a "bright" in the newspaper.

The brief item went on to explain that — following his usual custom — Baugh had made a small bet on the game with a teammate and had taken the opposing team on the theory that, "if we lost, the disappointment wouldn't be so bad if I won the wager. And if we won, I'd be so glad I wouldn't care about losing the money."

Recalling the mood of the era, Baugh laughs and says, "Hell, back then we did a lot of things that nobody gave much thought to. It was a time when you just kinda tried to make anything you were doing fun. I guess if you did that today they'd put you on probation or something."

At the time, however, there were a lot of people willing to pay Baugh money — not penalize him for earning it. And, the relaxed attitude of the time also extended to graduation ceremonies. By the time the class of 1937 donned its robes, its most prominent member was up in the Texas panhandle, playing ball.

"I never even waited around to get my grades that year," Baugh says. "The way I was figuring, I had finished school and it was time for me to get out and get a job.

"Mostly, you still thought that way in those days. Pro football was not something that was really on a lot of people's minds. Hell, at that time I couldn't have named any of the pro teams for you — and I had no idea how many there were, exactly.

"I really didn't know if I was ever going to play football again. I sure wasn't (against) playing some more, I just never thought about it. What I really thought about a lot more was baseball."

ALL-STAR ENCOUNTER

And so, Baugh was soon an infield fixture with the Pampa Roadrunners — a semi-pro team that was headed for a memorable engagement.

"They played a lot of different teams — any kind of barnstorming team that came through," Baugh says, "and there were a lot of them traveling through the panhandle back then."

"One deal they used to do every year was play in this tournament — I think it was in Denver — where this team of black all-stars always came in to play."

So, on one unforgettable afternoon, Baugh and the Road-runners found themselves facing a black all-star team that included Satchel Paige, Josh Gibson and Cool Papa Bell.

"It's a game I'll never forget," he says, "because we had a damn riot.

"It all started when Bell hit a ball into the outfield that looked like it was going into the gap.

"But the center fielder managed to knock the ball down and make a throw in to second base that had Bell beaten. But he came in with his spikes high and hit the second baseman and knocked him backward about seven yards.

"So our second baseman is lying there with blood running down his face, and all of a sudden both benches emptied. I never saw anything like it — guys were coming out of both dugouts carrying bats, and pretty soon they were all in a big crowd swinging at each other.

"I was just trying to get out of the way, and so was the pitcher. So pretty soon the two of us were standing out there at shortstop just holding onto each other. I was amazed nobody got killed, but we did have one guy that had a broken arm.

"Anyway, it pretty much broke up the game."

It is Baugh's recollection that the man who was spiked was Sam West — but since West was then employed by the St. Louis Browns, it may have been his brother, Ned.

HORNSBY'S LATEST FIND

More significant than the riot, however, was the fact that Baugh was "discovered" by Rogers Hornsby, who was then managing the Browns and scouring the country for potential talent.

After being fired by the Browns later in the season, Hornsby touted Baugh to Branch Rickey, who subsequently signed him to a contract with the Cardinals.

Eventually, Baugh went to spring training with the Cardinals in 1938 — but there were problems, one of which was that he had become one of the biggest stars in the National Football League.

"Well, first off, when Hornsby saw me, I was playing shortstop," Baugh says. "I forget why — maybe our shortstop was hurt, but I think it was because they had signed a third baseman who used to be in the big leagues, so they moved me over.

"Anyway, when Hornsby saw me I was playing the wrong position, and the Cardinals never knew the difference. I guess I played pretty well — but my real position was third base. But I never got to try out there. I met a lot of those guys who had been in the Gashouse Gang, and I played some in Columbus. But pretty soon, I figured out that my future was probably in football and not baseball.

"One reason was that I'd already played a season in the NFL and gotten a raise because we won the championship. The Cardinals told me that if I really wanted a career in baseball, I would have to give up football, and I didn't want to do that.

"Another pretty good reason was Marty Marion — he was in their farm system by that time, and it was obvious that he was gonna be their shortstop of the future. After watching him, I knew there was no way in hell that I would ever beat him out at short.

"So, it all ended up just being kind of a fun thing to try — but after that, I stuck to football and I have never regretted the decision."

It is interesting to speculate what might have happened if the Cardinals had tried Baugh at third. In the late 1930's and early 40's, the Hot Corner in St. Louis was manned by a collection of journeymen — Don Gutteridge, Stu Martin and Jimmy Brown — who were not destined for permanent residence. Had Baugh resolved his disagreement with the curve ball (or changeup), he might have had the major-league career he had once dreamed of.

Waiting in the wings, however, was the third baseman destined to help the Cardinals win four pennants and three World Series titles in the 1940's — Whitey Kurowski.

"And he said, 'If they're willing to pay that, ask for $8,000 and see what they say.'"

—Sammy Baugh

TIME TO PLAY FOOTBALL

But in relinquishing his once-cherished dream, Baugh launched a career that would ultimately stretch longer than any other in NFL history up to that time. As for its beginning, auspicious it was not.

Baugh, in fact, cannot remember now whether he was contacted by phone, telegram or letter — just that one day he received a message from the Redskins congratulating him on becoming their No. 1 draft pick.

"I didn't know what they were talking about," he says, "because frankly, I had never heard of either the draft or the Washington Redskins.

"The way they scouted back then was they read a lot of newspaper clippings, and I think some people from TCU may also have let them know about me. Anyway, I had just finished playing in the College All-Star Game — we beat the Packers, 7-0, and it was only the second time the pros had ever been beaten in that game.

"But I had also taken a hit on the sternum, and I wasn't feeling real good at the time. But George Preston Marshall, the owner, contacted me and offered me $5,000, so I went to see Dutch.

"I didn't know what to do — $5,000 wasn't bad, but I had a coaching offer out in Arizona, and I was thinking of taking it. I went and talked to Dutch, because he was kind of like a father to me, and I said, 'What should I do?'

"And he said, 'If they're willing to pay that, ask for $8,000 and see what they say.'

"So I asked for eight, and they agreed. That was more than the job in Phoenix (a high school coaching position) paid, so I signed with the Redskins."

Washington coach Ray Flaherty watches as Baugh signs a pro football contract to play for the Redskins in 1937. At the time of his signing, Baugh was the highest-paid player in the National Football League.

CHAPTER SEVEN

A Brave New World

Baugh's Unorthodox Style as a Washington Redskin Broke Pro Football Wide Open

On December 12, 1937, Wrigley Field seemed a more appropriate site for a gathering of penguins than the championship game of the National Football League.

As a howling wind swept across a field slick with ice, Wrigley's patrons ignored the numbness in toes and fingers while patiently waiting for the most forlornly frozen group in the stadium to disintegrate.

This would be the Washington Redskins, backed up to their five-yard line and seemingly on the verge of being swallowed whole by the fearsome Chicago Bears.

It was at this juncture that Sam Baugh, the Redskins' rookie quarterback, walked into the huddle, looked around, and said, "OK, we're goin' into punt formation."

As his teammates began to break the huddle, he added, casually, "Then we're gonna throw the ball."

At a distance of 60 years, the memory of that moment still causes him to break into a wide grin.

"I sure got a few weird looks on that one," he says.

But in a few moments, he was being hailed as a bold pioneer, brilliant innovator, and all-around stout fellow.

Baugh took the snap, faded back into his end zone, and threw the ball to running back Cliff Battles, who turned it into a 42-yard gain that launched the year's most improbable scoring drive.

Rocked back on their heels, the favored Bears were further stunned in the third quarter when Baugh threw touchdown passes of 55 and 78 yards to Wayne Millner and 35 yards to Ed Justice to lead the upstart Redskins to a 28-21 victory and the league title in their very first year in the nation's capital.

By the end of the day, Baugh had completed 18 of 33 passes for 335 yards — a record that stood for decades — and established himself as the game's most dangerous heretic.

It has also often been said that on that day, he changed professional football forever.

USHERING IN THE MODERN ERA

It is in any case a fact that a game that until then had been a bruising test of strength became progressively more oriented toward the quick-strike, wide-open passing game that turned a struggling enterprise into a dominant aspect of American culture. The modern game began with Baugh and his gambling style.

"Aw, it was just a screen pass," he says, of the famous flip from the end zone. "It was just that it was something nobody would have thought of doing at that time.

"When I first came into the league, they didn't want you to pass. Everybody tried to win by running the ball, and nobody knew a damn thing about the passing game. Throwing from that deep in your own end of the field was unheard of.

"But Dutch would have loved it.

"One thing I have to say, though — the main thing I remember about that game was that it was so cold I could barely grip the ball. That day in Chicago, that was the worst field I ever played on."

The 1937 season, at any rate, was an immense success for the Redskins and their new star quarterback — who was now launched on a spectacular 16-year career that would eventually land him a spot as a charter member of the Pro Football Hall of Fame.

"He was just an immediate success, from the first day," says Sam Boyd, who came into the league with Pittsburgh in 1939 after an outstanding career as a receiver at Baylor. "What he did that first year, especially, pretty much destroyed the notion that every quarterback had to be 'seasoned' for a few years before he could hope to make it as a pro.

"From the first time he stepped onto the field, Sam was the best quarterback in the league — the best there ever had been. And in all my years of playing and coaching, I still can't think of anybody I ever saw who could throw the ball like he could."

It was also in 1939 that Dick Todd, the former Texas A&M star, joined Baugh in Washington. It was the beginning of a lengthy professional relationship for the two men — both as players and coaches — and a lifelong friendship.

In Boyd's view, it also made the Redskins twice as hard to handle.

"When I joined the Steelers," he says, "everybody in the league up there knew about Sam, because he was the top quarterback in the league and everybody prepared for Washington by trying to stop him.

"I knew all about Dick, because I'd played against him for three years, but nobody else up there had ever heard of him. The first time we played Washington, I tried to tell our people that we needed to watch out for the new running back. But they told me, 'We don't worry about rookies.'

"Well, early in the game we had them backed up on their four-yard line, and all of a sudden Sam takes a snap and just straightens up and throws a quick slant to Todd, who runs 96 yards for a touchdown.

"After that, they paid a lot more attention to the rookie."

A REUNION OF SORTS

By that time, the Philadelphia quarterback was Davey O'Brien — fresh from guiding TCU to the 1938 national championship.

And while Little Davey had achieved the ultimate in college football — winning a national championship and the Heisman Trophy after having once been Baugh's understudy — his pro career paled in comparison with that of his old teammate.

O'Brien played only two years with Philadelphia — a dreary franchise constantly trying to pin itself together — then retired from football and launched a distinguished career with the FBI. Sharing his misery in 1940

was another ex-Frog, end Don Looney.

"We were pretty pitiful," Looney says. "The successful teams then were the Giants, Redskins, Bears and Packers, and the rest of us were just hanging on. I always used to hope they'd trade me to Washington so I could go over there and play with Sam and Dick Todd, but they never did.

"We were always short-handed and banged up, and everybody just played hurt. We never had much of a line to protect Davey with, because there were always people missing.

"I remember one game where we suited up three guys who couldn't walk, just so we'd have some people on the bench. One guy had a broken leg, and we just carried him out there and sat him on the bench."

By the time the final game of the 1940 season rolled around, O'Brien had had enough. But there was one last great game still in him — and it came against Baugh and the Redskins.

"I remember I went over and talked to him before the game," Baugh says, "and he told me that this was going to be his last game. They just couldn't protect him, and he was getting beat up really bad.

"But he sure went out in style."

In the last NFL game he ever played, O'Brien set records that would stand for years by completing 33 of 60 passes — including 14 to Looney — even though the Eagles lost the game, 13-6. Among those defending against his passes was Baugh, who was a two-way player for much of his career.

"I saw a lot of Sam that day," Looney says. "I'd go out and catch a ball and then I'd hear Sam hollering at me, congratulating me on the catch. They'd already clinched the division title, and he was having fun.

"Once when I caught a pass, Sam went over and started complaining loudly to the official that I'd trapped the ball, but the guy wouldn't listen to him. Then when he was going back to his position he trotted by me and grinned and said, 'Nice catch.'"

UNPREDICTABLE OWNER

The NFL at that time was a fertile domain of

vagabonds playing for $75 a game — when they felt like it — trainers who carried an adequate supply of liquor to soothe aches and pains, and various characters with undetermined histories. But there were strange characters everywhere, not least among them being George Preston Marshall, the owner of the Redskins.

He had scored a great coup in 1937 by signing Baugh and moving his team from Boston, where it did not draw. Baugh brought success both on the field and at the box office, and Marshall tirelessly promoted him as the West Texas cowboy (which, after 1941, he was) who befuddled defenses as "Slingin' Sam." Countless interviews and photo sessions were set up featuring Baugh dressed in western boots and hat. The search for Old West story angles was diligent:

Reporter: "Sam, is it true that you once shot and killed a buffalo?"

Baugh: "Naw, I just winged him."

But while he treated Baugh well, "beloved" was never a word used to describe Marshall.

Baugh, at the Polo Grounds in New York City, during his rookie year in 1937.

"I always got along with him pretty well," Baugh says, "but he was always doing crazy things, and most of the guys didn't like him worth a damn. I think while I was there he fired three coaches in the middle of the season, and finally he talked Todd into finishing out one of those years as coach. He was unpredictable, and not well liked by anyone.

"One time, we had this great tackle named Fred Davis, and Marshall traded him to the Bears. So we had to face him in several championship games and he always got a big kick out of beating us.

"I signed with the Redskins because he gave me a contract for $8,000, which at the time seemed like a million

bucks. And in a way, it was.

"After I had been on the team awhile, I discovered that we had three All-Pros making $2,700 each. And there were a lot of other guys — veteran players — making $150-200 a game. I mean, we had some of the best players in the league (Baugh, Battles, Millner and Turk Edwards are now in the Hall of Fame), and they were making nothing.

"It scared the livin' hell out of me, because I was afraid they might find out how much I was making and kill me. It made me feel really strange to know I was so overpaid when we had guys doing their job just as well as I was and making less than $200 a game.

"We had a great year and won the championship and Battles led the league in rushing, and so he asked for a $300 raise up to $3,000 a year. And Marshall wouldn't give it to him, so he quit.

"Hell, if I'd known about it, I would have given him the $300 myself, because after that first year I was making $12,000. When we won the championship, Marshall called me in and insisted that I sign a three-year contract before I went back to Texas.

"It was a lot of money for that day and time, so I signed it. But hell, I never paid that much attention to the salary, and in the years after that I don't remember us talking much about it."

THE 73-0 ROUT

Marshall, however, was also adept at behaving badly even when money was not the issue. In Baugh's view, the most memorable instance of this remarkable trait played a major role in the most hideous defeat any team has ever

The Redskins' 1940 backfield (left to right), Frank Filchock, Andy Farkas, Sam Baugh and Dick Todd, prepare for their NFL Championship game against the Chicago Bears.

Joe Stydahar (13) of the Chicago Bears gathers in a Sam Baugh (33) fumble. The Bears would defeat the Redskins, 73-0, in the 1940 NFL title game played at Griffith Stadium.

suffered in an NFL Championship game — Chicago's 73-0 massacre of Washington in 1940.

Late in the season, the Redskins defeated the Bears, 7-3, in a hard-fought struggle in Washington, and Marshall immediately began crowing. He ridiculed the Bears and called them "crybabies" for their post-game remarks about the defeat.

With Chicago enroute to the Western Conference championship and Washington winning the Eastern Conference, a rematch was inevitable, but Marshall wouldn't let up.

"Everywhere he went, he would talk about it," Baugh says. "He just kept making fun of them every chance he got. It was ridiculous for anyone to say stuff like that

about a team that was as powerful as they were back then. Year in and year out, they were the strongest team in pro football, and everyone knew it.

"Every time Marshall opened his mouth, they got madder and madder, and our morale got lower and lower. He basically destroyed his own team, but George was like that. I never knew anyone who liked him much.

"Anyway, they started scoring early and never let up, and we couldn't do anything right. When it got to be 28-0 in the second quarter, I went over to our coach, Ray Flaherty and told him we might as well go for broke, because we didn't have a chance anyway. So we started throwing on fourth and 10 instead of punting, and things just got worse.

"I remember saying, "Hell, we may get beat, 60-0, but we've got to try it.' Well, we sure didn't get beat 60-0."

The rout was launched when Bill Osmanski ran 68 yards on Chicago's first play from scrimmage, and the Bears later ran three interceptions in for scores, as 10 different players crossed the goal line. By the end of the game, Chicago had kicked so many extra points into the stands that there was only one football left for the teams to play with, and the officials prohibited any further kicks.

The rout did at least give Baugh an opportunity to deliver a deathless post-game quote.

Early in the game, a Washington receiver dropped a sure touchdown pass in the end zone. Sensing a "momentum shift" angle, reporters trooped into the locker room afterward and asked Baugh how he thought the game might have come out if the receiver had caught the ball.

"73 to 6," said Baugh.

CRAZY CAST OF CHARACTERS

But, while Marshall may have brought disaster to his own club, most of the NFL's bizarre characters were simply entertaining. And on the Redskins, one stood out among the crowd: Wee Willie Wilkin.

"He was a big ol' lineman out of St. Mary's, and a helluva football player, when he wanted to be," Baugh says. "He was extremely fast for a lineman, and he could also punt the hell out of the ball. He was one of the most valuable players we had, most of the time."

But what Wee Willie did best was enjoy himself. Thoroughly.

"They had a bunch of boys out there playing for the Bears who were a lot like Willie," Baugh says, "and they all got along real well. I don't remember us ever making a trip to Chicago where Willie wasn't missing when we boarded the train to go back to Washington. He would always stay out there a couple of days and drink with those guys.

"One time, he stayed out there a whole week. Our practice schedule back then was maybe not quite as regimented as what you find today, and all through the week we kept working out but there was no Willie.

"He finally showed up on the day of the next game, about an hour before the kickoff. He came stumbling into the locker room, and God, he was a mess. His clothes were all wrinkled like he had been sleeping in them for a week, and he was in pretty bad shape.

"He stumbled over to his locker and started getting undressed, and we were all laughing and trying to help him out, but it was slow going. Finally, our coach, Ray Flaherty, walked in and there was Willie, trying to keep from falling over backward off the bench, with one pants leg on and one shoe on the wrong foot.

"Ray walks over there and looks at Willie, and he was so mad he was just speechless. He stares at him for a minute, then he just hauls off and slaps the hell out of him.

"Willie goes tumbling over backward onto the floor, and he's laying there and his feet are still up on the bench, and he looks at Ray real forlorn like, and says, 'Aw, coach — I came in here today real fired up and ready to play the game of my life for you.

'And now, you've done gone and broke my spirit.'"

WEE WILLIE TAKES THE PRIZE

Wee Willie was a great friend of man and beast, regardless of political affiliation, social standing or choice of beverage. He would befriend anyone with a spare shower.

"I ran into him out on the coast one time," Looney says, "when we were out there for some kind of charity game or something. Willie was in a room at the hotel right across the hall from me, and he comes over and knocks on the door and asks if he can come in and take a shower.

"I said, 'Sure,' figuring something must be wrong with the shower in his room. Then I went over there a little while later and found out why he didn't want to use his own shower. He had the tub filled to the top with iced-down beer."

Wilkin distinguished himself on another occasion when the team was staying in a rather uptown hotel, whose patrons were prone to parade their pedigreed pets through the lobby each morning.

"We used to get a big kick out of watching that," Baugh says. "Then one morning we're standing in the lobby watching this — and Willie comes prancing through the front door, and he's got this dirty, frayed old rope tied around the mangiest, scruffiest mutt you ever saw — who immediately starts growling and yapping and attacking every dog in the lobby, and there was this big panic, but we were all rolling on the floor, laughing."

But finally, Wee Willie fell in love.

"One year," Baugh recalls, "Willie went back to California after the season and met a woman who was traveling through with the migrant workers, picking grapes. She was a really impressive woman — nearly six feet tall and kinda rough-looking, but she and Willie hit if off from the start, and pretty soon they got married.

"When he brought her back to Washington for the next season, some of the other players' wives were a little apprehensive because she looked and acted kind of ... different.

"They had these regular get-togethers where they would all sit around and drink coffee and talk — and the first one of those she attended was really something.

"They were all sittin' around talking and smoking their cigarettes, but they sort of quieted down when she got there. She walked in and kinda gave 'em all the once-over, never cracked a smile, and then walked over to the table and sat down.

"She looked around at all of 'em for a minute, kinda of tough-looking, then reached in her purse and pulled out some papers and a sack of Bull Durham and sat there and rolled her own. She licked it and then pulled a match out of her pocket, hiked up a leg, struck the match, and then sat there puffing away.

"Some of 'em nearly fainted, but it turned out she was just having fun with them. She knew they all thought she was a little strange, so she put on that act as a joke.

"As time passed, we all got to know her real well, and she was one of the nicest people I ever met."

But in the NFL of that era, this was all pretty much normal business.

Boyd recalls that he once became a holdout over a salary issue of $15 per game — and lost his head coach in the same manner that the Redskins periodically lost Willie Wilkin.

"One year I signed with Pittsburgh," he says, "and

On a return trip home from the NFL, Baugh visits with former Horned Frogs teammates, Johnny Vaught (right) and Bill Walls.

they offered me $185 a game, which was pretty good at the time. The going rate for linemen then was about $125 per game. But the really amazing thing about it was it was a no-cut contract, which was practically unheard of.

"But some of the people coming into the league then were getting a little more money for signing, so I told them I wanted $200 per game. They didn't want to give it to me, so I held out.

"Finally, Mr. (Art) Rooney had the coach call and tell me I could have the $200, but they were taking back the no-cut contract."

The Pittsburgh coach at the time was one of the more memorable characters in the history of the league. His real name was John McNally, but he became enshrined in NFL legend as the famed Johnny Blood.

"The way he got that name," Boyd says, "was that one day, a young woman handed him a pen and paper and asked for his autograph. On a sudden whim, he pricked his arm with the pen and signed his name in blood — and that's how he became Johnny Blood.

"He had been one of the really great players in the 30's, and I knew a great many guys who had played with him for years and thought that was his real name. He was a real character."

Also, like Wee Willie, he thoroughly enjoyed visiting those fun-loving Bears.

"Shortly after I signed my contract," Boyd says, "we went out to Chicago to play the Bears, and when we got back on the train, John wasn't with us. He stayed out there for a couple of days partying with the Chicago players, and Mr. Rooney became so furious that he fired him."

BAUGH TAKES MATTERS INTO HIS OWN HANDS

Meanwhile, the league was slowly changing — partly due to the drawing power of quarterbacks like Baugh, O'Brien and the Bears' Sid Luckman. In 1938, roughing the passer became a 15-yard infraction.

"They used to chase you down regularly and put you on the ground after you threw the ball," Baugh says. "At first, I didn't think much about it, until they gathered us together one time and showed us a film someone had taken of our last game.

"There was a play where I threw a pass for about 15 yards and the receiver made a few extra yards after catching the ball — meanwhile, their linemen were chasing me all over the field even though the play was elsewhere. When the play was over, me and the receiver were both on the ground — 70 yards apart.

"After that, they started changing the rules."

By this time, however, Baugh had devised his own method of diffusing the unduly enthusiastic pass rush.

"In one game," he says, "there was a guy who kept coming in on the rush, and every time I threw, he brought his hand down and hit me in the face.

"The other guys wanted to run a 'bootsie' on him — which is a play where everybody on the team jumps on one opposing player and works him over in the pileup. But I said 'No, I've got a better idea — just don't trouble him on this next play. Let him come on in.'

"On the next play, he came charging in and I drew back and threw the ball as hard as I could. The point of the ball caught him square in the forehead, and I guess that leather headgear compressed and cut off the oxygen or something, because he just suddenly stopped dead still and his arms fell limp at his sides, and his eyes kind of rolled. He teetered there for a minute and then keeled over, and I thought, 'My God, I've broken his neck.'

"But in a few minutes they revived him, and he even came back into the game later on. But they were a little more careful about the rush."

One of the most versatile players who ever lived, Baugh generally kept the Redskins at or near the top of the league standings through his ability to pass, punt and play defense as well as anyone around. And although Todd, Looney and many others went off to serve in World War II, Baugh was exempted because he was in his late 20's with a growing family back on the ranch in Rotan by the time the war started.

In 1942, the Redskins and Bears were back in the title game, this time with a markedly different result.

Coming in at 11-0, Chicago was a 22-point favorite but managed to score only once — by picking up a Washington fumble and running it in.

Baugh quickly retaliated with a 38-yard scoring pass to Wilbur Moore, then guided the Redskins 56 yards for third quarter TD to complete the scoring in a 14-6 game. Doing his part in an outstanding defensive effort, he then intercepted a pass at his 12-yard line to close down the final threat by the Bears.

In 1943, Baugh led the NFL in passing and punting and also picked off 11 enemy passes from his safety position to lead the league in that category as well. The Redskins parlayed this into another Eastern Conference championship, but it wasn't easy.

"We had some guys back from injuries that year and we had a pretty good team," Baugh says. "But we ran into one of the strangest situations I ever saw.

"We had a two-game lead with two games left in the season, and looked like we were in good shape. But both of those games were with the Giants, who were in second place.

"It was a strange deal, and I don't know if there's ever been another time when two teams were scheduled to play each other two weeks in a row that way.

"Well, we went up to New York and they beat us (14-10), but that didn't worry us much because we figured we'd win the next game at home. Then they came down to Washington and beat us even worse (31-7), and that really got our attention.

"In fact, it pretty much demoralized us. Here we'd had a comfortable lead, and now they'd whipped us twice and we were forced into a playoff situation where we had to go back up to New York and play them again.

"The Giants always played tough defense, and now I figured they also had the psychological advantage. It looked like our season was finished."

But in the third game, in New York, Baugh took care of Washington's miseries almost single handedly. He completed 16 of 21 passes for 199 yards, directed four scoring drives, and intercepted two Giant passes as the Redskins overwhelmed their hosts, 28-0.

"That was a thrill," Baugh says, "but I still think it was weird we had to play those guys three weeks in a row."

At that point, they probably should have declared the season a success and gone home. Rested and confident, the Bears buried the Redskins, 41-21, in the title game as Luckman threw for five touchdowns and accounted for 350 total yards.

RULES CHANGES COME TOO LATE

Late in the season, Baugh had received a visit from an old TCU teammate, Judy Truelson, who was an assistant coach on the strong Iowa Pre-Flight team that had just lost a national championship in a late-season showdown with Notre Dame.

"I had been sent to Washington on some kind of military business, so I decided to go by and see Sam," Truelson says. "I got to the Redskins' practice field, and there was a trainer airplane sitting out front that had a top speed of maybe 75 miles per hour.

"There was a sign on it that said, 'This is the plane Sam Baugh uses to fly back and forth to his ranch in Texas.'

"When I saw Sam I asked him if this was true, and he just started laughing and said, 'I wouldn't go near that thing on a bet, let alone fly it. It's just another of George's promotions.'"

As the war wound down in 1945, the Redskins again reached the title game — this time against the Cleveland Rams, soon to be relocated in Los Angeles.

In a rather bizarre affair, Washington fell behind, 2-0, when Baugh, throwing out of his end zone, saw his pass bounce off the goal post and fall out of bounds.

"Under the rules of that day," he says, "that counted as a safety. It's about the same thing that happened to me in the Sugar Bowl 10 years earlier when an LSU player batted one of my passes out of the end zone. That also counted as a safety.

"In both cases, they changed the rule the next season, but it didn't do me any good."

Later, an extra point kick by rookie quarterback Bob Waterfield barely made it through after caroming off the upright, as the Rams won, 15-14, dashing Washington's hopes for another NFL title.

It marked the fifth time in the nine years that Baugh had been the quarterback the Redskins played in the championship game of professional football. It would not happen again for 27 years, when the coach would be George Allen and the president of the United States would be Richard Nixon.

For the near future, the heyday of the Washington Redskins was over.

CHAPTER EIGHT

A Chief Among Redskins

Quarterback Sam Baugh Continues to Display Class as Pro Career Winds Down

In the autumn of 1947, the most feared power in the National Football League's Western Conference was, as usual, located in the Windy City. There was, however, a twist. This time, it was not the Bears but their cross-town rivals, the Cardinals. It was, in fact, a time of modest upheaval in the NFL, and the old power base of Bears-Packers in the West and Giants-Redskins in the East had begun to erode.

For a while, the new kingpin in the East was Philadelphia — but the most amazing transformation occurred with the oft-lowly denizens of Comiskey Park, who had recently come through the war with a total of one victory in three years.

There, in lightning fashion, Jimmy Conzelman constructed a sudden juggernaut that rolled through the 1947-48 seasons with 21 victories in 26 games, two Western Conference titles, and an NFL championship. Its centerpiece was the famed "Dream Backfield" of Paul Christman, Pat Harder, Elmer Angsman and Charley Trippi.

At the end of the 1947 season, Conzelman's team would defeat the Eagles, 28-21, for the NFL title, with Angsman contributing a pair of 70-yard touchdown runs and Trippi scoring on runs of 44 and 75 yards.

But on November 23, the unsuspecting Cardinals rolled into the nation's capital and became the featured entree in a festive little ambush called "Sam Baugh Day."

By now, the Redskins' peerless leader was in his 11th professional season, and in honor of a decade of thrills

---

Baugh (33) angles in to tackle New York Giants fullback Bill Paschel at the Polo Grounds in 1943.

and triumphs, Washington turned out to honor "Slingin' Sam."

He was presented with a new automobile, the usual keys to the city, and a variety of other gifts. But the finest gift of all came from his teammates — who gave him the Chicago Cardinals, dead on a plate.

"It was one of the most amazing things I ever saw," he says. "It was our last game at home that year, and I knew the brass had set up that 'Sam Baugh Day' thing, but I didn't give it much thought.

"The Cardinals were the best team in pro football, and they had that great backfield — every one of them had been an all-American in college, and they were doing great with the pros. We had one of our poorest teams (4-8) ever, and they figured to run all over us.

"But the team had had a meeting and formed a plan, except nobody told me about it until right before the game.

"As we were walking out to the field, one of the tackles came up to me and said, 'Don't worry about a thing — you'll never hit the ground today. Nobody will touch you, you won't even get your uniform dirty. That's a promise.'"

At first, Baugh was startled.

"I thought he was crazy," he says, "but I'll be damned if they didn't do exactly what they said they would. They went out there and whipped the Cardinals, I mean just whipped them, and nobody touched me all day."

Never one to accept a gift ungraciously, Baugh responded by completing 25 of 33 passes for 355 yards and six touchdowns. As a stadium full of Redskins fans whooped and screamed with glee, the Cardinals were buried, 45-21.

"Y'know, most of the time I never paid much attention to awards and records and 'big' games and that kind of thing," Baugh says. "I always figured you just went out there and did your job every time, and if you did it well, things would fall into place.

"But I remember walking off the field after that game thinking, 'This is one day I will always remember, and someday, it's really gonna mean a lot to me.'

"And that's true.

"But there's something else that came out of that, that I always think about: that game convinced me once and for all that football is all right up here in your head.

"Those guys were so much better than us it was pitiful. Be we were just determined to win that game, and they never had a chance. It's all mental, and if you want to do something bad enough, you can do it.

"I often think about what we could have done if we'd played every game the way we played that one. ..."

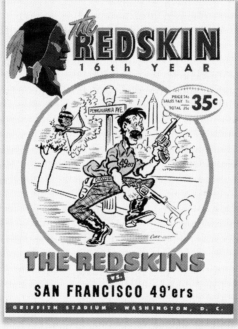

TIDE TURNS FOR THE NFL

Unfortunately, such performances became increasingly rare as the franchise marched steadily through the post-war world to a position of prolonged mediocrity.

Or, as Baugh once put it, "I played on some really great teams up there, and I also played on some mediocre teams ... and I played on some really sorry ones."

There were a variety of reasons for this, but the most obvious was that it was simply part of the natural ebb and flow of fortunes in the NFL, coupled with the explosion of new franchises after the war and the tremendous influx of new college talent warming up to a business that was finally paying decent money.

The emerging medium of television soon gave the NFL its golden opportunity. The end of Baugh's career coincided with the beginning of the sport's transforma-

tion from a cold-weather substitute for baseball to a billion-dollar business that finally reached areas of the world where the average citizen does not speak English.

By 1950, the NFL had brought in the stronger members of the All-America Conference and reached the markets of California. For the teams that had dominated the close-knit league of the 1930's and 40's, it was an unstable, new world.

It would be many years before anyone again referred to the once-mighty Bears as the "Monsters of the Midway," and after Don Hutson retired, the Packers endured many years of losing prior to the arrival of Vince Lombardi. The Giants experienced periodic success, the Redskins periodic hope.

By the time Baugh retired in 1952, the Eastern Conference was being thoroughly dominated by the Cleveland Browns, a team that had not even existed in 1945.

There was also Marshall's continuing game of Russian roulette with the coaching staff. Ray Flaherty, who coached Washington to two NFL titles, left after the 1942 season. He was replaced in 1943 by Dutch Bergman, who was replaced in 1944 by Dudley DeGroot, who was replaced in 1946 by Turk Edwards, who was replaced in 1949 by John Whelchel, who was deposed at midseason in favor of Herman Ball. Dick Todd was pressed into service in 1951, and Curly Lambeau arrived in 1952.

Another major change had occurred in 1945, when the Redskins scrapped their traditional double wing for the new T-formation — at first with spectacular results.

In 1945, Baugh had what in a technical sense was his greatest season — completing 128 of 182 passes with only four interceptions to establish club records that still stand today for completion percentage (70.3) and quarterback efficiency rating (109.7).

As the years went by, the offense became less productive, but Baugh still managed to throw 25 touchdown passes in 1947 and capture his sixth and last NFL passing title in 1949.

On December 11th of that year against the Rams, Baugh recorded his eighth 300-yard passing game. It would be 13 years before anyone wearing a Washington uniform would reach that plateau again.

A MENTOR AND A FRIEND

And in his "declining" years, he was still a sight to behold — especially for the two young quarterbacks brought in to be groomed as his eventual replacements.

Shortly after Baugh returned to his ranch after the 1947 season, he got a phone call from Marshall.

"I just wanted to let you know," he said, "that we're going to sign Harry Gilmer out of Alabama."

"Fine," said Baugh.

"And also, that because of the bonuses these kids are getting today, we're going to have to pay him more money than we're paying you."

"Well," Baugh said, "So?"

It was a conversation that in later years Gilmer found to be typical of Baugh, whose only concerns about money involved paying off his ranch.

"Actually, my salary that year (1948) was only $10,000, which was not more than Sam's," Gilmer says, laughing. "But it's true that with the signing bonus, I made a few thousand more than he did. But it was only for one year."

Like Baugh, Gilmer was an extremely versatile player who had had no collegiate experience with the T-formation — having gained fame as a passing wizard out of the Notre Dame Box at Alabama, where he twice nearly led the Crimson Tide to the national championship.

"When I signed with the Redskins, Mr. Marshall told me they were bringing me in to be Sam's understudy, with the idea that eventually I would be the next quarterback," Gilmer says. "The idea was for Sam to train me and for me to study everything he did.

"So I started studying Sam, and the first thing I learned from that was that I wasn't going to be the quarterback of the Washington Redskins anytime soon."

The second thing Gilmer learned was that, far from being resentful over the arrival of his "replacement," Baugh was happy to welcome a new member of the group.

"It was amazing just to stand around and watch him," Gilmer says. "From that time forward, I stayed in pro football a pretty long time — about 27 years, as a player, coach or in some capacity. I saw a lot of passers come and go, and Sam was as good as any I ever saw.

"He wasn't a real good runner because he was actually slow — but he had real quick feet, and he could take a couple of quick steps and move around back there and evade the rush.

"I was with the Redskins for the rest of the time that Sam was there, and I really can't remember ever seeing him sacked. I suppose he was, but I don't recall it. That was always a big important thing with him, because he felt that every time he got sacked, he let the team down. He was an expert at getting rid of the ball if he had to — but he usually got it delivered.

"And he was incredibly accurate, just like a great pitcher is always on the money throwing strike after strike."

Gilmer arrived in the league at a time when it was still customary for quarterbacks to invent plays in the huddle — an option Baugh used as well as anyone.

"He could be very innovative," Gilmer says, "especially when he had Todd around. Those two had been together so long they had developed that rapport where each knew instinctively what the other was thinking. Many times, Sam would throw to a spot and Todd would suddenly arrive to catch the ball — to the complete surprise of the defenders. Sam was kind of ahead of his time, in many ways."

> *"He could start telling stories, and you'd get up on the edge of your seat — and two hours later he'd still be telling stories and you'd still be sitting like that."*
>
> *—Harry Gilmer*

Gilmer also became the latest in a long line of observers awed by Baugh's punting, even though he was no longer the team's regular punter.

"By that time, Mr. Marshall had decided he didn't want Sam to punt anymore, because he was afraid he would wear his legs out," Gilmer says. "It was kind of silly logic, because Sam punted every day, anyway. It was the way he warmed up.

"I'll never forget this one routine where Sam would hold a football and get some of us to form a circle, and then we would start running around the circle, and he would be running around and he would kick the ball to you. It amazed me, because he always kicked it right into your hands.

"But every once in awhile, he would kick in a game, and he was fantastic. You know, he still holds the NFL record for that year where he averaged 51.4 yards per kick, and he also holds the career record (45.1). With the modern game and the prolonged season, they've broken all of his passing records, but those two may stand for awhile.

"But it was a different style of kicking. Nowadays, they want as much height on the ball as they can get. They try to kick it high, and they kick it straight downfield, over the goal line. Nobody tries to kick it out of bounds anymore.

"By comparison, Sam's kicks were more like low line drives, and he never kicked it down the middle of the field. He would kick to one side or the other, angling for the out-of-bounds stripe.

"That technique also created a kind of interesting phenomenon — the other team would always put a double safety back there. The only times I ever saw anyone use a double safety were when Baugh was punting."

84

A CHIEF AMONG REDSKINS

FOND MEMORIES

But in Gilmer's eyes, Baugh's exploits on the field were overshadowed by his personality. In the late 1940's and early 50's, the Redskins were losing more than they won, but the kid from Alabama was having a ball.

"They used me at quarterback a lot, as Sam's backup," he says, laughing, "but nothing he could teach me was going to make me as good as he was. They used me at running back because I had played in the single wing, and I was a starting halfback one year when Choo-Choo Justice got hurt. Then when Eddie LeBaron came along, I had to move to defense if I was going to play (Gilmer and another former Alabama tailback, Ed Salem, led the team in interceptions in 1951).

"Finally, they traded me to Detroit because they wanted an older guy to back up Bobby Layne.

"But I have such fond memories of those years in Washington, and it's all because of Sam Baugh."

Gilmer was soon hanging around with Baugh and Todd, and the group picked up a fourth member when the Redskins traded for Bullet Bill Dudley.

"Sam pretty much adopted me right off," Gilmer says. "Actually, he could get along with anybody, and usually did. He was a straight-shooter — anything you asked him, he told you exactly what he thought, no matter what. But he was also one of the most entertaining people I've ever known.

"He could start telling stories, and you'd get up on the edge of your seat — and two hours later he'd still be telling stories and you'd still be sitting like that. And he and Todd together could keep a crowd going for hours."

Marshall's endless promotion of Sam Baugh the Slingin' Cowboy was still going strong, and Gilmer recalls that "he was always arranging things — I think one time they had a big to-do for Sam down in Sweetwater — and he always made sure Sam had a $100 Stetson and new boots.

"I've always thought it was funny because I've visited Sam down there on that ranch several times, and every time I go down there he's walking around wearing a baseball cap.

"But of course, he really was a rancher. Pretty soon we started sharing an apartment because neither of us took our wives to Washington, and one place where we lived had a kitchen table with some chairs around it.

"Sam would sit there for hours with that rope of his and lasso one of the chairs. He would turn the back of it away from him — like he was roping a calf — and toss that rope around it over and over. Whenever anyone came to visit, one of the chairs was usually lying on its side with a rope around it."

LeBaron, the man who finally did replace Baugh, has a slightly different recollection.

"After I joined the team," he says, "they invited me over one night. When I got there, they handed me a blanket.

"I walked in and the place was dark, with some candles burning, and freezing cold.

"I couldn't believe it — they were living in an old abandoned building just a few blocks from the White House. They had no heat, no electricity, no running water. I think Todd or Dudley was living in there with them, too. They were kind of a strange bunch."

The recollection brings a howl from Baugh, who says things weren't as bad as LeBaron thinks. They may have been worse.

"What it actually was was a hotel they had emptied for renovation," he says. "We went over there — I guess it was me and Gilmer and Todd — to see about renting, and they explained that they were remodeling the place.

"But we kept talking to them, and finally they said they had a few rooms ready that they could rent, and they could give us a discount. So we took it.

"There were two sisters who lived down the hall from us, and we got to know 'em pretty well. Since none of us had our wives in Washington, they decided to cook Thanksgiving dinner for us, so they cooked this huge ham for us and brought it over.

"So we all sat down and had this big meal — but it was such a big ham that we couldn't eat it all. After awhile, someone says, 'What are we gonna do with the rest of this?' And so to get it out of the way, we just stuck it in the oven.' Then we forgot about it.

"When we came back the next year, we went back to that hotel. Now they were fully renovated and open for

business and the place looked really high class, but they gave us a discount again — and put us in the same room.

"So we move in, and pretty soon we open the oven for something — and there's the ham, still there."

COMPASSION FOR OTHERS

In 1948, for the last time in Baugh's career, the Redskins had a decent team — finishing second in the division at 7-5.

"One of the biggest things about Sam," Gilmer says, "is that he is a person who really cares a lot about other people. He never tried to advertise the fact or make a big deal of it, but he just really cares about folks.

"That year when we finished second, it meant we were in for a little extra money, because in those days the second-place team got some shares even though it wasn't in a playoff or anything.

"So somebody called a team meeting, and they were sitting around discussing how to divide it up. And there was some guys who had gotten hurt and hadn't played much, and some of the others wanted to cut them out of the pot and keep those shares to divide for themselves.

"Sam sat there and listened to this for awhile, then suddenly he gets up out of his chair and looks around and says, 'What the hell are we talking about here? Those guys are our teammates, and they're just as much a part of this team as any of the rest of us. They just had some bad luck, and we didn't!'

"That pretty much quieted down the meeting, and everyone on the team wound up with an equal share."

The two quarterbacks concluded their professional relationship in 1965-66, with Baugh serving as an assistant to Gilmer at Detroit. But they have remained close friends through half a century.

"The last time I went down there to his ranch, I got there about two o'clock in the afternoon, and we sat down at the kitchen table and started talking," Gilmer says. "At 10 o'-clock that night, we finally stopped talking and went to bed."

Baugh and Redskins equipment manager Kelly Miller pose for a publicity photo in front of the Capitol.

Of Baugh's forays into the NFL coaching ranks in the 1960's, Gilmer laughs and says, "Y'know, Sam never wanted a full-time coaching job, which is why he kept resisting when people tried to make him a head coach. He just wanted to be an assistant, so he would have time to go home once in awhile.

"But I'll promise you, a lot of Sam's thinking went into the way I coached all those years."

LEADER BY EXAMPLE

In 1952, the Redskins were finally ready to make a change at quarterback with the arrival of LeBaron, the 5-foot-7 dynamo who in 1949 had driven tiny College of the Pacific to a No. 10 national ranking. Now returning from a stint in the Marines, he was ready to take over the job.

It was a momentous occasion: the last time someone other than Baugh had held the starting job for an entire year, the franchise was located in Boston.

But before LeBaron could launch a new era in Washington, he had to acclimate himself to the endearing ways of the old one.

"The year I joined the team," he recalls, "Dick Todd started out the season as the head coach. But at halftime in our first exhibition game, he quit.

"He just got upset about something, but he never said anything to us. Just sent us out to the field for the second half, and then went home. And he never came back."

Hastily, the Redskins hired Curly Lambeau to replace Todd — by which time LeBaron was becoming intrigued with the ancient warrior he was about to depose.

"The guy was in his 16th NFL season," LeBaron says, "and he was amazing.

"He was the best thrower I ever saw. He was very fluid, and he could throw overhand, sidearm, off balance, and hit a guy on the run wherever he wanted to. It was incredible — here was this guy winding down at the end of his career, and he was phenomenal.

"There was another thing — when I came in as a rookie, they told me they wanted me to do the punting. Then I walked out on the practice field and watched Sam warming up, and I had to wonder about our choice of kickers.

Baugh was a popular hero in his hometown of Sweetwater, Tex., after the Redskins won the 1937 NFL title.

"He would line up five guys down at the other end of the field and kick the ball to each of them. If you had to move a step or two to catch the ball, he figured it was a bad punt."

Although LeBaron was not invited to move into the plush accommodations near the White House, he, like Gilmer earlier, found Baugh to be a most affable and helpful Senior Legend Figure.

"He was always very nice, very helpful," LeBaron says. "There was basically a lot of difference in our techniques, and he never had a problem with that. He was not the sort to jump out at you with all kinds of instruction, but anytime he said something, you listened.

"I hadn't been with the team very long when he came over one day, draped an arm around my shoulder, as said 'Son, don't try to do what I do. Do what you do.'

"It was good advice."

PASSING THE BATON

With the diminutive LeBaron paired with the 6-foot-2 Texas rancher, Marshall now had another publicity gimmick, and endless Mutt and Jeff photos began appearing in the newspapers. But there is something else that stands out in his mind about his relationship with Baugh.

"Sam was a great passer," he says, "and a really exceptional field leader.

"In those days, the quarterbacks had a lot more say in what was going on than they do today, and Sam basically invented the Washington offense. I think Curly knew about three plays, and that was it.

"But it was a T-formation offense, and he had never in his life had a coach who actually understood it. It just became the offense one year, and Sam had adjusted — but no one had ever coached him at it.

"The one thought I always have about Sam is that I wish he could have played for a coach who understood that offense. If he had played for Paul Brown, he would have been so far out there that nobody would have ever broken his records. It's mind-boggling to speculate on what he could have achieved playing for Tom Landry."

But, although he graciously endured an evening wrapped in a blanket in a dark apartment tossing off bon mots with his fellow strategists, LeBaron does harbor one complaint about his first year as a Redskin.

"The setup in our locker room in those days," he says, "was that the quarterbacks — Sam, Harry and me — were off in one area by ourselves, and about six feet in front of the lockers there was a drain.

"Sam and Harry both chewed tobacco, and all the time we were dressing they would spit into that drain. Consequently, every home game we played that year, I was sick before the kickoff."

In the first game of Sam Baugh's 16th season, a prearranged plan was set in motion.

"Sam started the game," LeBaron recalls, "and played the first half.

"He threw 11 passes and completed every one of them. And in the second half, I became the starting quarterback of the Washington Redskins."

Baugh puts on Redskins jersey No. 33 for the last time prior to the 1952 season finale against Philadelphia.

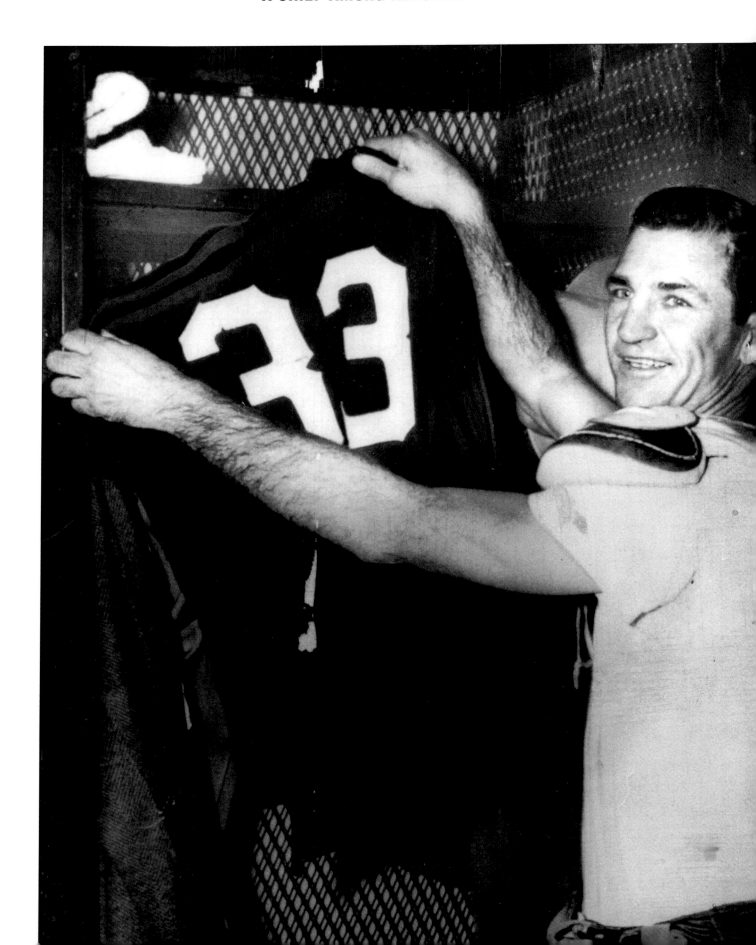

CHAPTER NINE

A Tough Assignment

Baugh's Coaching Jobs Ranged from Ridiculous to Impossible

In 1953, the National Football League opened the season without Sam Baugh for the first time since Alf Landon challenged Franklin Roosevelt for the presidency and Adolf Hitler began expanding his new German state.

In the wake of the departing Texan was a mind-boggling collection of records and achievements and a legacy that has now survived nearly a half century.

Baugh, however, was not quite ready to lay football aside.

"During my last two years at Washington," he says, "I was helping out coaching the quarterbacks, and during the spring of 1952, I got a call from Murray Evans, who was the coach over at Hardin-Simmons.

"He said, 'Why don't you come over and help us with spring training? It would be a big help if you could work with our quarterbacks.'

"So I said OK, and I went down there and did it. I liked him real well and I really liked those boys, and I enjoyed the whole thing.

"That fall, I went up to Washington and played my last season, and he called me again in the spring.

"I got to thinking about it, and I realized I really wasn't ready to get out of football — and I had always kind of thought about coaching, anyway. So they hired me as an assistant coach."

Things went swimmingly for a couple of years, and then Evans quit.

"The athletic director came to me and asked me if I would take the job," Baugh says. "I was happy doing what I was doing, and I had never really thought about being the head coach. But he was persuasive, and we had had a real good recruiting year, so I agreed.

"Then he said, 'There's one thing I need to tell you — I want to upgrade this program and have us play the toughest opponents we can find. So I've scheduled several teams out of the Southwest and Southeastern conferences for the next few years.'

"So I said, 'Fine, whatever you want.'"

And so, in 1955, Baugh became the head coach of the Hardin-Simmons Cowboys — one of three feisty "small college" teams located in Abilene, which was one of the reasons he took the job.

"It was a pretty good deal, really," he says. "It was only an hour and 10 minutes from the ranch, so I could be the head coach and still commute, and I could keep an eye on things at the ranch."

OUTGUNNED IN COLLEGE RANKS

At the time, Hardin-Simmons was a member of the Border Conference — which included, among others, Arizona, Arizona State, New Mexico, Texas Western (now UTEP), and the Cowboys' then-arch rival, Texas Tech.

In this environment, the Cowboys had more than held their own for decades. Under Warren Woodson in 1946, they had gone 11-0, and in the late 1940's and early 50's, the SWC had held several votes on the question of bringing H-SU and Tech into the league in tandem. They were well-respected — and often feared — from Lubbock to Tempe.

They were also fighting a losing battle against the tide of history. When Tech was accepted, alone, into the SWC in 1956, the Cowboys celebrated the event by smashing the Red Raiders, 41-14, in the season finale. But by 1958,

After retiring from pro football, Baugh became the head coach at Hardin-Simmons College in Abilene, Tex.

Head coach Sam Baugh and New York Titans management line up to take on the New York Giants.

they had disappeared from the Tech schedule — forever.

With increasingly limited financial resources, Hardin-Simmons made one last, desperate bid for big-time football glory in the late 1950's. It meant playing seven to eight games a year on the road, but with history's most famous quarterback mapping the offense, it was a wild ride.

Featuring quarterbacks such as Ken Ford and Harold (Hayseed) Stephens, the Cowboys could always move the ball. But they faced a withering succession of Top-20 teams that proved, in the end, to be more than they could handle.

Baugh's first opponent as head coach in 1955 was Bay-

lor, which was coming off a Gator Bowl season. In 1956, it was Arkansas. In 1957, the Cowboys faced an Ole Miss team that went 9-1-1 and smashed Texas, 39-7, in the Sugar Bowl. In 1958, they played Baylor, LSU, Mississippi and Arkansas. On successive weekends in 1959, they met an Auburn team that had just suffered its first loss in 24 games and an Orange Bowl-bound Georgia squad led by Fran Tarkenton.

In the course of these adventures, Baugh made the acquaintance of a fellow TCU alum and distinguished southern gentleman — Johnny Vaught.

"A very gracious man," Baugh says. "I'll never forget

Johnny and those Ole Miss teams. God, they were awesome.

"They could have beaten the piss out of us, but Johnny held the score down."

But the highlight of Hardin-Simmons' crusade to hang with college football's elite came on a steamy evening in Baton Rouge. Awaiting the Cowboys in Tiger Stadium was the team destined to win the 1958 national championship, featuring a charming band of social misfits known as the "Chinese Bandits."

Awaiting the assembled Tigers, Bandits and howling fans was a fairly harrowing battle — courtesy of Sam Baugh and the Dutch Meyer Deluxe ball-control passing game.

"I got to admit," Baugh says, grinning, "we played 'em pretty good. Of course, the thing you have to remember is that it's impossible for a great team like LSU to get up for Hardin-Simmons. They took us lightly, and we took advantage of it."

The final score was 20-6, but without a pair of key sequences, the Tigers might have found themselves deadlocked going into the final moments.

"With about a minute and a half left before halftime," Baugh recalls, "we snapped the ball over our punter's head, and they recovered it for a touchdown. Then in the second half, we drove downfield and they finally stopped us on about the one-yard line. That's a 14-point swing that could have made it a very interesting game.

"During the offseason, I got a call from one of their assistants — I think it was Charlie McClendon — and he said, 'I just thought you'd like to know, we've been looking at the film from last year's games, and you controlled the ball on us better than anyone else we played.'

"Actually, we followed a real simple plan the whole game — throw about a seven-yard pass on first down, then use two running plays to get three yards and move the sticks downfield. We knew it was the only way we could sustain a drive against them and use up the clock. And it worked."

But by the time the Cowboys ran into Georgia in 1959, the gas tank was getting low.

"We ran into Auburn just after Tennessee had beaten them," Baugh says, "and they beat us pretty bad (35-12). The next week, we had a lot of people banged up

After two seasons as the Titans' head coach, Baugh stepped down to become an assistant with the Houston Oilers of the AFL.

and limping when we went to Georgia, and they beat us bad, too (35-6).

"In the offseason, Harry Wismer called me and said he had a team in the new American Football League called the New York Titans and asked if I would come coach it.

"And I said, 'You're damned right I will.'

"All in all, it was a move I look back on with regret. Those years at Hardin-Simmons were among the happiest I ever had. But Wismer was offering me about $28,000, and in those days, that kind of money was hard to turn down."

Its energy spent, Hardin-Simmons won three games in the next four years and then erased football for 26 seasons. Under the circumstances, Baugh's 23-28 record for five years ranks as a considerable achievement. The Cowboys finally revived the program in 1990 under Jimmy Keeling, who has created a spirited NAIA Division II powerhouse.

A TOUGH ASSIGNMENT

UNDER-FINANCED IN THE PROS

In 1960, meanwhile, Baugh found himself coaching the albatross of the American Football League.

When Lamar Hunt launched his new conference with the ambitious — and ultimately successful — aim of challenging the entrenched National Football League, the key New York franchise was awarded to Wismer, who had coast-to-coast name recognition as a famous sportscaster.

All began well, as the league secured a television contract and Wismer acquired the right to use the Polo Grounds for home games. Unfortunately, he did not have the deep pockets necessary to survive the early years.

"That was one of those things that was just a bad deal from the start," Baugh says. "In the beginning, we all thought Harry owned the team, but actually he had no one backing him up. We started losing money fast, and he couldn't cover it."

With former Michigan State star Al Dorow at quarterback and Texas Western's Don Maynard as the go-to receiver, Baugh's team was never at a loss for offensive firepower. Paying customers were another matter.

On Sept. 11, the Titans stepped off smartly, burying Buffalo, 27-3. Rattling around in the Polo Grounds was a throng of 10,000 — of which 5,727 had actually bought tickets.

"That was our first problem," Baugh says. "The Polo Grounds was a bad place to play — old and dirty. But at least we never had to worry about hostile fans, because we always had 'em outnumbered."

Baugh coached the team for two seasons, compiling a 7-7 mark in each. Dorow completed 398 passes for 5,400 yards — and in 1961 the Titans could balance Maynard on one flank and Art Powell on the other. But the defense and the owner were rapidly sliding downhill.

"Harry," Baugh says, "was one of those guys who seemed to go out of his way to be his own worst enemy. Frequently, you'd see Harry doing things an ordinary man doesn't need to be doing.

After Pop Ivy quit as head coach of the Oilers, Baugh took over the coaching reins for the 1964 season.

"He was always big-doggin' it. He was the kind of guy who would walk into a restaurant and yell at somebody on the other side of the room, just so everyone would turn around and look at him.

"He was always coming into the dressing room trying to give us a pep talk that nobody ever listened to. It was embarrassing just to be around him, and before long a lot of people started hating him."

There were worse problems, however, than Wismer's personality.

"The paychecks were bouncing," Baugh says, "and that'll sure create a little unrest on the team. Every time we got paid, everyone would tear out the door and run to the bank — 'cause they knew the last ones in line would have their checks bounce."

As for personnel, Baugh says, "signing Maynard one year and Powell the next was the best thing we ever did. Other than that, an awful lot of guys came through camp. We would literally look at anybody."

At the end of the 1960 season, Baugh recalls, the Wismer Bonus Rule went into effect.

"Things were pretty bad, and morale was low," he says, "so one day Harry walks into the dressing room and announces that if we win the last three games on the schedule, he'll pay everyone a $2,000 bonus.

"Since a lot of guys hadn't been paid in weeks, this got everyone kinda fired up.

"Well, we won the first two, and then went out and played the Chargers in the last game of the year. We could both score, and it got to be one of those real seesaw games — we'd score, and then they'd score. Harry was pacing up and down the sideline looking more worried every minute.

"And all through the game, people were joking with each other on the bench — pointing at Harry and saying, 'Look — we got him scared to death!'

"Finally, they beat us (50-43) — and you never saw an owner so relieved his team had lost."

LOSING MORE THAN JUST A GAME

By the end of the 1961 season, home attendance had dropped below 15,000 per game and the list of Wismer's creditors had grown to include the coaching staff. So Baugh accepted an offer from Frank (Pop) Ivy and became an assistant with the Houston Oilers.

"The next year, when Bulldog Turner was the coach up there, Harry ran out of money," Baugh says, "and the league took the franchise away from him."

The following year (1963) a syndicate headed by Sonny Werblin paid $1 million for the franchise, changed the name to the "Jets," and hired Weeb Ewbank as the coach. Two years later, the team laid out an unheard-of $427,000 for Joe Namath — who in 1968 led the Jets to a Super Bowl title.

Within a span of four years, thanks to Namath, the franchise was generally credited with forcing the NFL to the merger table and then proving on the field that the AFL was legitimate. Harry Wismer became one of history's forgotten men.

"I actually felt sorry for Harry about the way he lost the team," Baugh says, "because he was just in over his head and it never was quite fair. But there were a lot of people who really despised him.

"The year after he lost the team, I was with the Oilers and we were up there playing the Jets — and Harry called me and asked if he could come down and sit on the bench with us. I said sure, and I got him a pass.

"So he came and sat with us, and it seemed like it really meant something to him. But at halftime, he went up to the pressbox to go visit some people.

"About the middle of the third quarter, he came back down, and he had blood all over his mouth and running down his shirt. He went up there big-doggin' it again, and somebody cold-cocked him.

"There were just so many people who disliked Harry, and I really felt sorry for him."

In Houston, meanwhile, a familiar scenario occurred.

"Right before we started the 1964 season," Baugh says, "Pop Ivy quit. They came to me and asked if I would coach the team. I agreed to do it, although I didn't want to.

"I coached that one year, and then the next season I asked them to just make me an assistant coach again. So they agreed and hired Bones Taylor. I really just wanted to be an assistant coach, so I would have a chance to come back to the ranch occasionally. Being the head coach was a full-time job."

END OF THE LINE

After playing in the first three AFL title games and winning two of them, the Oilers began to slide downhill in the mid-1960's amid coaching changes and quarterback controversies.

"They had drafted Don Trull out of Baylor as their quarterback of the future," Baugh says, "and I think they may have been pressing Ivy to play him immediately, and that was maybe why Pop quit. I was willing to work Trull in some, but we had one of the best quarterbacks in pro football in George Blanda, and he was obviously our starter.

"Bud Adams, the owner, was also interested in Namath, but I heard that Namath told Bud he would only play in New York. We also had the (AFL) rights to Jerry Rhome out of Tulsa, but the Cowboys outbid us."

Baugh's fondest memory of Houston concerns Blanda, the man who erased his longevity record.

"We were playing Denver once, and Blanda had had a great day and we had 'em beat with about two minutes to go," Baugh says. "Then our punter decides to run with the ball instead of kicking it, and he gets caught behind the line of scrimmage, and they take over and beat us with a field goal.

"The newspapers jumped all over Blanda, even though it wasn't his fault, and I think Mr. Adams may have instigated it because he wanted Trull in there.

"So the next game, against the Chiefs, we started Trull and we were behind, 21-0, at the half. George came in in the second half and threw five touchdown passes, and we ended up beating them.

"After the game, the writers were all crowded around Blanda's locker, but he had his back to them and wouldn't turn around and talk to them.

"They kept trying to ask him questions, and finally he turns around and snaps, 'You guys know so damn much about it, just write whatever the hell you want!' And he turned back to his locker, and that's all he ever said to them."

After that year, Baugh left Houston. He spent one year coaching the Oklahoma State freshmen, and a couple of seasons helping Harry Gilmer in Detroit.

But by the time the 1960's came to a close, Baugh was back on the ranch in Rotan — for good.

CHAPTER TEN

Home on the Range

Sam Baugh Passes on Bright Lights of Fame for the Rugged Life of a West Texas Rancher

The two peaks rise out of the flat, endless West Texas plain like a pair of chiseled monuments to the whim of some capricious god, who stuck them there just so people would wonder why.

Although he climbed them for years, Sam Baugh has never figured out just how high they are. Somewhere up on the nearest one, there's a rock monument with the elevation, but it has become weathered to the point that no one can read it.

It never mattered much, really. For more than half a century, the great quarterback has counted them as friends. Even now, when he can no longer climb them, it is an immense comfort just to know they are there.

They are called the Double Mountains, and for 56 years they have formed the back gate to the 7,667-acre spread north of Rotan on which Baugh and his late wife, Edmonia, raised five kids, thousands of head of cattle,

After joining the Redskins, Baugh starred in the movie serial "King of the Texas Rangers."

and countless memories.

They are noble and esteemed edifices that have provided geographical bearings for miles in all directions, dating from the time when most in this country traveled on horseback. The nearby fork of the Brazos River is named after them.

And in all the years they have sat two miles from his back door, Baugh has never lost the ability to gaze at them in wonder.

"Y'know," he says, "you can look at 'em from different directions and they seem to change shape. They look like different mountains from the west than they do from the east. I guess it sounds pretty damn silly, but that's always fascinated me.

Indeed, the westernmost of the two appears, from some angles, to be twin peaks, due to a saddle in the middle. The other, closer to the ranch, levels off in a wide plateau, strong and sturdy like the people who settled the land.

"The first time I ever saw 'em was in 1941, and I fell in love with them," Baugh says. "That's when we bought this place, and I've never wanted to live anywhere else."

When he bought the ranch, Baugh was already being hailed as possibly the greatest quarterback who ever lived — spending his autumn Sundays entertaining huge throngs in the nation's largest cities, on his way to becoming the highest-paid player in the NFL at the time.

He had even starred in a brief movie serial called *King of the Texas Rangers*, in which he spoke a few lines and did a lot of riding (he was paid $4,500 for six weeks' work).

But none of it, exactly, fulfilled the boyhood dream he had never relinquished.

"Ever since we had had that farm in Temple, I had always loved living in the country," he says. "And I always loved riding horses and fooling around with cattle.

"After we moved into town, I used to go out and visit this boy whose family had two or three horses and some diary cows. We would go out in the pasture and milk the cows, and it meant we got to ride the horses around, and I loved it. I was always volunteering to help that kid milk the cows.

"All the time afterward, I always thought that if I ever

had the chance, I'd like to get me a little piece of land with some horses and maybe some cattle. And after I started playing with the Redskins, that's what I was looking for."

PRIMITIVE BEGINNING

By the time he found it, however, Baugh wasn't sure the entire family was all that thrilled with it. The charm of the Double Mountains had its drawbacks.

He and Edmonia — high school sweethearts — had married in 1938 after his first season with the Redskins, and their first child, Todd, was born the year they moved to the ranch.

"The first year we were married," Baugh says, "I bought a little place on Sweetwater Lake, and that's where we lived.

"There was a man who owned a place with about 750 acres on the east side of the lake and he wanted to sell, so I bought it. I think Edmonia liked it pretty well — it was a nice place with all the conveniences and it was close to her family and all. But it wasn't a real ranch, and it wasn't what I wanted.

"There was a man named Mr. Dennis who lived out here then, and he heard I was looking to buy a little land so he contacted me and I came out here with him to look at the place.

"That's when I first saw those mountains — and the closer we got to them, the more I knew this was where I wanted to live.

"But the place was a lot different then. I mean, there wasn't a damn thing here — just a four-room house with no running water and no electricity. It was real primitive ... so I never really said much to Edmonia about it.

"I borrowed the money to buy it from a woman over in Eastland that I never met. It was arranged through a lawyer in Abilene, Carl Springer, who found her and made the deal. It took a long time, but I paid her back every cent."

And so, the famed meal ticket of the Washington Redskins became a genuine West Texas rancher — with his own piece of the wild scrub and cattle country that someone once dubbed "The Big Empty."

Years later, his bride confided to a visitor that she had

The Baugh family on the ranch in Rotan, Tex., prior to the birth of Frances.

originally regarded it as "a temporary jumping off point" — and had never dreamed that she would spend the rest of her life there.

Baugh says he had doubts that she would last the first year.

"To tell you the truth, I never thought she'd stay out here," he says. "It was real primitive, even for me. But I was used to not having much.

"It was especially hard on Edmonia — she had a real rough time. Her father was a Presbyterian preacher, and

she had always lived in the town (Sweetwater). She wasn't used to this.

"When I told her I had bought the place, she said, 'Fine, we'll move out there.' But she didn't know what it was like.

"We had to use (oil) lamps in the house because there was no electricity. All the water we ever had — for bathing, cooking, everything — came from a cistern. And in a lot of dry years, there wasn't much.

"A lot of times, we bathed in the horse trough. And

Edmonia used to do the washing in a big black pot out in the yard. She really worked hard.

"This was the kind of place I had wanted since I was a little kid, but I put us in a lot of debt to get it. I was making pretty good money playing football, but between paying off the mortgage and trying to keep cattle on the place, it was a few years before we had enough to make improvements on the house.

"Really, paying the bills on this place was the main reason I played all those years with the Redskins. The first couple of years, she used to come up and we would rent a place over in Silver Spring (Maryland) — but after that she had to stay home and raise the kids. There were times back then when I wondered why she stayed."

When Edmonia died in 1990, she had lived on the ranch for nearly 50 years, and she and Sam had been married for 52.

WRESTLING WITH THE ELEMENTS

In that time, life in palatial West Texas proved to be a continuous education.

"The year we moved out here," Baugh says, "one thing that really amazed us was how much it rained. We had some Hereford cattle, and the rain brought the grass up so well we were really excited.

"During one stretch, it rained seven Sundays in a row, and by the end of the year we had had 43 inches. We were thinking this was really going to be easy.

"Back then, we didn't own all the land that's around here now, and you had to go through seven wire gates to get up there to the farm road, and you'd cut across other people's property.

"One day I went through there and I stopped to visit this guy — old man Kennedy — who lived over there. We were sittin' there on his porch talking, and I mentioned how much it had rained, and how happy we were with it.

"Well, he kinda smiles and then he says, 'Son, I've been out here since '03, and I've never seen this much rain before. And you'll never see it again.'

"Damned if he wasn't right."

Sam and Edmonia soon learned that the normal weather patterns were much different than they had been in that first year — often near-drought conditions.

"One thing you learned early was not to build up your herd too much," Baugh says. "If you stocked too many head, you'd end up losing a lot of 'em."

It remains a fact of life today, says Baugh's son, David — who essentially divides his time between coaching the Snyder football team and managing the family's two ranch properties. For the last 35 years, the Baughs have leased a second piece of land a few miles away.

"We've had a lot of rain this year," David says, "but last year we had drought conditions and we had to try to sell off everything we could. So now we're running about 450 head, whereas we normally run about 600."

Citing a second recurring feature of the business, David notes that "the bottom fell out of the (beef) market."

When World War II arrived, Baugh — by then 27 years old — was exempted from military service because he ran a producing ranch. But the ranch and everyone on it might have starved had it not been for that handsome NFL salary.

"The first calf crop we brought in, we sold for nine cents a pound," he says. "By then I was learning that ranching was a little harder than it had seemed to be when I was a kid."

As America rolled through the war and the boom period that followed, Baugh became the highest-paid football player in the country — which is to say his salary eventually reached the $20,000 plateau.

But with paying off the mortgage, buying more land, raising five kids (Todd, David, Bruce, Stephen, Frances) and dealing with the peaks and valleys of the cattle business, the Baughs usually found use for every dime of it.

"For the longest time," Baugh says, "it seemed like we were always up to our ears in debt. But things smoothed out, eventually. Around 1950, we had the place fixed up enough so that Edmonia's mother came to live with us, and my mother also lived with us for 17 years.

"But it was hard — real hard — on Edmonia back in the beginning when we didn't have the conveniences. It wasn't the kind of life that people raised in the city are used to. I was usually off trying to make more money, playing or coaching. She stayed here and ran the ranch and raised the kids."

A PLACE TO RAISE CHILDREN

But if it was sometimes difficult for the grown-ups, it was an idyllic existence for the younger Baughs.

"I've always felt that I had a great childhood — about the greatest you could have," says David Baugh. "I lived out there on that ranch, with all that land and the livestock and the wildlife that was around — and I loved it. There was always something for a kid to do. I do remember going out to the outhouse when I was young, but that never bothered me.

"I went to a small high school where the teachers kept a check on you and made sure you learned what you were supposed to.

"Nobody around here ever made a big deal about us being Sam Baugh's kids. To other people, he's a legend, but to me he was just my dad. Every year he would go off for several months to work, but for a long time I was never that conscious of what he did.

"One year late in his career, my mother took me to

While shooting "The King of the Texas Rangers" serial over a six-week period, Baugh earned $4,500.

Washington to see him play. But the main thing I remembered about it was seeing all those historical monuments.

"I think my dad was probably a definite influence on me in what I wound up doing, but probably the greatest influence in my life growing up was my mother.

"My mom was a great lady — and all those years she was always ready to do anything at all for us kids. She was always positive about everything, always looked on the bright side, never got discouraged.

"She was in a class by herself."

Frances, the only girl, was the last to arrive — being born shortly before Baugh retired from pro ball.

"We set out to raise two boys and a girl," Baugh says, laughing, "but it didn't work out that way. Those two youngest boys — whenever I had trouble with them, I used to tell them, 'Just remember — you're lucky she didn't come along right after David, 'cause if she had, you two wouldn't even be here.'"

For Frances, memories of life on the ranch echo those of her brother.

"It was an ideal existence," she says. "Being out here in the country was one of the big attractions, and we all loved it. Anything my brothers did, I just joined in because I didn't want to be left out. I got a few bloody noses playing baseball, but that didn't matter.

"As far as my dad was concerned — he was just 'daddy' to me — not some famous celebrity. The first time I really became aware of what he did was when he was coaching with the Oilers, because I was in high school by then.

"When he would come home, my mother would make us go to him whenever we wanted something. And usually, he would say, 'Well, what did your mother say?'

"He was just really easy-going, laid back — except when he got to a certain point, and then you knew you'd better do what he told you to do.

"But of course, we always had my mother there when we needed something. She raised us, and she was the sweetest, most big-hearted person you could imagine, and she did everything for us. It was hard on her when the water froze up — but she would deal with it. Often she would make three or four trips a day into town, hauling us to various activities we were involved in. She went to all our football games, basketball games, or whatever.

"She was the most wonderful mother you could ever have."

Also, clever enough to turn her eldest — Todd — into the local heavy.

"When my dad was gone, Todd was the disciplinarian," Frances recalls. "Whenever my mother had trouble with any of us, she would get Todd to handle it. He was the oldest and he had a paddle that he used to spank us with. He put notches in it, and he could put welts on you, and we were all terrified.

"We used to scheme about getting that paddle and burning it — but he kept it hidden so well we never could find it."

LIVING WITH WILDLIFE

In addition to the livestock, the ranch always had its share of wild creatures — including coyotes and even turkeys. Although he has sometimes sold leases to hunters, Baugh never took much interest in it himself.

"I always used to like to watch the wildlife, but I've never fished or hunted or shot a bird on this place," he says. "One time, there was a herd of antelope out here, and I used to go up on those slopes and watch them. But one year the government let some deer loose out here, and the antelopes went west.

"But I always explored, and I loved going up those mountains. Usually I would climb up, but once I rode a horse up there.

"There was a trail you could follow, but all the way up, she was acting skittish, and I could tell she wasn't happy to be going up. When we got to the top, I found a patch of good grass up there, so I just dropped the reins to let her graze.

"I wandered on over to the point up there overlooking the bluff — and I was just enjoying the view when I turned around and noticed she was gone. She had just turned around and headed straight back down the mountain.

"I was chasing after her — but I never would have caught her except that she came to a rock in the trail and went around it the wrong way and got trapped in the brush, and I got on and rode her back down.

"If she'd gone around that rock on the other side, I would have had a damned long walk home."

CHAPTER ELEVEN

Sam Baugh's Greatest Legacy

Playing Records Aside, Legendary Quarterback Makes His Finest Mark as a Family Man

The blackboard in the coaches' office at Snyder High School looks pretty much like any other — with the X's and O's and sweeping arrows and cryptic notations. Except for the three words, in capital letters, in the lower right-hand corner:

"SHORT, SAFE, SURE"

And so, Dutch Meyer's offense lives on, in the hearts and minds of the Snyder Tigers.

It is hardly surprising, however, given the identity of the Tigers' head coach — David Baugh.

"Yeah," he says, grinning, "I think you could say my dad influenced my thinking a little bit."

But the similarities seem to run far deeper than the short passing game that has helped the Tigers gain three playoff berths in recent years despite having to contend with bigger, more powerful programs.

Now 53, Baugh has spent his entire life involved with football and ranching. He and his wife, Jean, grew up together (in the fifth grade, she moved eight miles away to Roby, but he kept track of her) and have been married 35 years, raising three children.

Like his brothers, he played football for the Rotan Yellowhammers (an egregiously feisty breed of woodpecker), graduating from high school in the spring of 1962. The next fall, younger brother Bruce played on a famed juggernaut that rolled unbeaten to the Class A state championship.

By the time David enrolled at Texas Tech, his mind was clear on the future — he had decided on coaching.

He played on a couple of bowl teams led by Donny

Anderson, and has now spent 30 years coaching high school football — all of it in West Texas. Starting at Lubbock Monterey, he moved through Levelland, Ralls, Andrews and Iowa Park before coming to Snyder — 35 miles from the ranch — in 1988.

Older brother Todd, a Rice graduate, is now a district judge in Montana. Bruce is in Austin, involved with the state's computer system. Stephen is with an oil company in Midland.

"They're all pretty smart," Baugh says, laughing. "I'm the dumb one who got into coaching."

After Edmonia's death, Sam began signing the ranch properties over to his children. He still owns the house and yard, overseeing a population of about a half-dozen dogs and cats.

The cattle spread he built over a period of 50 years is now run on a co-operative basis by his offspring — which has usually meant that David has made most of the immediate decisions, since he was the one living closest to the ranch until Frances moved back this year.

Sam is still regularly consulted for advice on matters concerning the ranch. For years after Edmonia's death, Jean brought cooked dinners over and stuck them in his freezer, but now Frances does most of the cooking.

Over the years, many have commented on the apparent similarities between Baugh and his second son — a pair of affable West Texans sharing a quick wit and a devotion to family, who have made a living off football and ranching. They frequently play golf together, and often seem more like pals than father and son. Nowadays, David usually refers to his father as "Sam."

But as time has passed, his appreciation of the man who was once "Dad" has stretched considerably.

"I guess it's a little surprising sometimes to watch the way other people react to him," David says, "and to re-

---

Baugh was selected to College Football's All-Time all-America Team in 1969.

alize that although you never thought of it that way, to them he's a legend.

"Growing up, we had my mother and a great life on a ranch, and we never felt deprived because our dad was gone a lot, making a living. The main thing I remember about that is that he always seemed sad to leave us.

"Now that he's been around for awhile, I have to admit ... he's pretty amazing."

One of Baugh's great friends, Melvin Diggs, once claimed that Sam had an I.Q. of 150. Although he probably never took an I.Q. test, it has long been recognized that the grin and the folksy drawl have sometimes tended to draw attention away from a very shrewd mind.

"After my mother died," David says, "I was over there cleaning out some things, and I came across a copy of his last contract with the Redskins. The figure on it was $20,000 or maybe $21,000, something like that. It's the most he ever made playing football.

"When you consider that and look at what he built here — it really is amazing. He did more with $20,000 a year than a lot of people do now who are making $5 million a year.

"A lot of 'em, you catch 'em a few years down the road and they're broke. My dad paid off a ranch, increased it, made it profitable, supported a large family, and never acted like there was anything to it."

MONEY CAN'T BUY HAPPINESS

For the children of The Great Depression, there is something that for more than six decades has coursed through their veins, lodged in the marrow of their bones, and shaped the perceptions of the mind — a determination to never live through it twice. Ironically, it has not made them greedy.

"There's a lot of things he could be doing now — autograph shows, celebrity appearances, things like that," David says, "but he's not gonna do it. Right now, he's living off his NFL pension and social security."

For Baugh, there is a simple logic to this: It's all he needs.

"Young people need money for a lot of things," he says, "but old people can get by on a lot less."

"After he retired from coaching," David says, "He came back and became a full-time rancher for about 15 years. By that time, of course, he had been calf roping for years and had traveled circuits to rodeos and other events. He did that until he hurt his knee and had to quit.

"My dad has always been one of those people that, every time he gets his mind set on something — football, ranching, golf — he throws himself into it and tries to become the best at it that there ever was.

"He's the most well-read man I've ever met — he's read everything from the Bible to the Third Reich; he's got hundreds of books over there, and he's read 'em all."

Baugh's lifetime achievements have not always been geared to a profit margin. But they have brought him the greatest gift of all:

"Basically," David says, "he's always been a person who is going to do what he wants to do, no matter what anyone else says. Pretty much, he has lived his life exactly the way he wanted."

It is a message that Sam and Edmonia made sure their children learned.

"I've had offers to coach in other places, for more money, and I won't say for sure that I would never leave," David says. "But it's true that I like West Texas. I like the country, and I like the people.

"But one thing my mother always used to say was, 'Don't let your paycheck determine where you live.' And I think we have always believed that."

'THE MOST COMMON UNCOMMON MAN'

As for life with a jovial and occasionally cantankerous legend, he laughs and says, "he has some eccentricities; we all have.

"A while back, the air-conditioning went out on his car, and he doesn't want to spend the money to get it fixed. I got in there the other day and it must have been 120 degrees inside. But Sam figures he lived a lot of his life without it, so he just opens the windows and heads on down the road.

"But if you want to sit down and talk to him, ask him a question, and you get an answer straight from inside him.

Baugh's TCU jersey was retired at halftime of the 1995 Horned Frogs-Texas A&M game.

Welcome Home, Sammy!

★

Sweetwater
Board of City Development Dinner

Honoring

SAM ADRIAN BAUGH
"Slingin' Sam"

Football's All-American World Champion

Blue Bonnet Roof

7 p. m.   December 20, 1937 $1.00

Sweetwater, '31-'32 . . . Texas Christian U. '34-'35-'36 . . . Washington Redskins 1937

"I remember once when I was coaching at Iowa Park, one of the writers there wanted to do a story on him. So Sam sat down and talked to him.

"Afterward, the guy came to me and said, 'Your father is the most common uncommon man I have ever met.'

"I've always felt that was a pretty good description."

Sitting at the kitchen table at the ranch, Frances casts a wary glance over her shoulder at three huge stacks of mail that lean against a wall and climb nearly to the ceiling.

"That thing fell on me the other day," she says, "and I said, 'Guys, we need to have a meeting and take care of this.'"

Periodically, Frances, David and Jean sit at the table, opening mail and passing it on to Sam to be signed.

There are numerous requests for appearances — the top item on the first stack is something from John Elway — and a variety of items to be autographed.

"He won't do it himself," Frances says, "but he will if we sit around and open each item to see what it is and then pass them to him. We have to do it every so often just to keep the stack down."

In an era when many celebrities place an outlandish value on their signature, Sam Baugh will give you an autograph for free — if you don't mind waiting maybe six or eight months for it.

At 46, Frances has rediscovered the lesson that your paycheck isn't your life.

She recently quit a job in the Lubbock school system and moved back to the ranch — partly to give her youngest son Cody, 15, a chance to go to high school in Rotan. She is also returning to the small town school system — to teach English and coach girls' basketball.

"I left when I was 18 to go to (Texas) Tech," she says, "and I've been in Lubbock ever since (teaching and raising two sons). But it's growing, and the schools are developing some of the problems you normally associate with larger cities.

"I wasn't happy with it, so I talked to my dad about coming back here and living on the ranch and working in the school system. It's been good for all of us — Cody loves it here, and it gave me a chance to get out of a job I hated. And I think I've been a help to my dad.

"Out here, this really is a wonderful life."

ENJOYING THE SIMPLE LIFE

It is a life Baugh decided he wanted when he was a little boy, riding a friend's horse to go milk a cow. Now, looking back on 60 years of it, he figures it has never let him down.

"I never liked cities," he says. "Any city.

"There aren't any big cities out here — just a lot of little towns. It does seem like there were more people around here when we first moved out here. There were a lot of migrant workers then, coming through picking cotton, and you couldn't stir 'em with a stick.

"But over the years, a lot of the farms and businesses have failed. It just seems like the place was bigger then."

One thing that is nearly the same is Baugh. He still weighs about 175 pounds — his playing weight.

About 15 years ago he got seriously ill after being poisoned by some cattle spray. He "swelled up like a toad" and nearly died, but he recovered. He doesn't recall having seen any doctor since then.

"I don't go much of anywhere," he says. "I just play a lot of golf (including his annual appearance at the Sam Baugh Invitational, which is held to raise money for golf programs in Snyder). I enjoy it, and it kinda keeps me fit.

"Old people need something to do. I can sit in front of the TV for three or four days, and I start feeling sick.

"But I get out and play golf, and it's exercise, and I start feeling better. I use the extremities, get the blood pumping, and have a lot of fun. When I come home, I'm hungry and I eat well. I'm also tired, so I sleep well. And I'm always home by dark.

"It seems to suit me. I don't take any medicine — not one damn pill — and I'm still a meat-and-potatoes man. I eat the same stuff now I've been eating all my life."

It seems to Frances that he has mellowed, that he enjoys visitors more. But the list of old friends is rapidly dwindling.

He has had many, in his time.

When they were young, they stood side-by-side and turned the football world on its ear with Dutch Meyer's baffling offense, built an improbable dynasty in the nation's capital, lived through a depression and a world war.

They laughed at hardship and believed they would be young forever.

Now, most are dead ... and many of those who remain can no longer make the journey to the ranch. At the mention of a name, Baugh says, "He's real, real sick, and I worry about him. I haven't seen him in awhile.

"Or you know, he's ... the best friend I ever had."

To those who played with him, Baugh was always "The best there ever was." To all who have known him, he has been a great and sincere friend. Most of it has always seemed something he never much thought about.

But for 83 years, he has enjoyed the ride.

"I guess I've seen a lot of changes," he says. "You know, when I was growing up in Temple, there were more wagons than automobiles. Sooner or later, everything changes.

"I'd kinda like to come back in 50 years and just see what's going on."

Then, his gaze stretches across the scrub to the two massive shapes, looming in the dusk. He smiles, as if checking on a pair of old friends before turning out the light.

"Hell," he says, "I'd like to do it all over again."

Then,

his gaze stretches across

the scrub to the

two massive shapes,

looming in the dusk.

He smiles,

as if checking

on a pair of old friends

before turning out the light.

"Hell," he says,

"I'd like to do it all over again."

Sam Baugh's
Ten
to Remember

Baugh Throws Passes Like Baseball Hurler to Shut Out Bears

By Flem R. Hall

Fort Worth Star-Telegram

WACO, Nov. 2, 1935

On the impulse of some the most accurate, spectacular and effective passing ever played on a football field, Texas Christian University walloped the previously undefeated Baylor University Bears, 28-0, here Saturday afternoon as 10,000 spectators looked on in open-mouth amazement.

But it was pitching — not passing. With Slingin' Sam Baugh doing most of the hurling, the Christians threw strike after strike past the dazzled and befuddled Bears for all four of the touchdowns.

The victory was the seventh straight for the Frogs and swept them in front of the fast-thinning ranks of the nation's major teams which haven't been beaten or tied. It was also their third conference win and held their place at the top, one win ahead of SMU.

Two of the touchdowns were scored in the second quarter and the other pair in the final 15 minutes. All were on passes — the first one, Jimmy Lawrence to Willie Walls; the second, Baugh to Rex Clark, and the last two, Baugh to Charley Needham. All the passes except the one caught by Clark on the four-yard line were completed deep in the end zone. The play on which Lawrence tossed to Walls started from the Baylor 12. The others were from the 34, nine and 15, respectively.

TCU threw 24 passes and completed 15 for gains totaling 204 yards. Baugh was on the throwing end of 16 of the passes and completed 10 of them. Lawrence, Manton and Montgomery were the other pitchers.

Passing was not all the Frogs' sweet junior quarterback from Sweetwater did. He carried the ball eight times for 40 yards; he did most of TCU's excellent punting and safety work. If he made any mistakes in the selection of plays, it couldn't be detected from the press box.

Baugh wasn't the only hero of the game that broke the hearts of thousands of Baylor exes here for homecoming, but he stood out so that the others will soon be forgotten.

Playing better than it has in any previous game, the TCU line — bolstered by Drew Ellis at left tackle held the Bears to only three first downs on running plays. Capt. Darrell Lester, Tracy Kellow and Wilson Groseclose were most prominent in the middle of the forward wall. Coming back to his last year's form, Walter Roach led all the ends (L.D. Meyer, Melvin Diggs, Walls, Needham and Snow) in an afternoon of great work — work that resulted in Baylor losing almost as many yards as it gained by rushing, 35 to 42. Lloyd Russell, Baylor's ace, lost 18 yards while gaining a total of five.

The closest the Bruins came to scoring was the 24-yard line.

The game was played on a dry but spongy field, and under a partly cloudy sky. There was practically no wind and the temperature was up around 75 degrees.

Baugh completed 10 of 16 passes for three touchdowns and ran for 40 yards on eight carries.

The big, white team started piling up its 18 first downs as soon as it got the ball but, after marching 50 yards deep into the Baylor end of the field, it lost a scoring chance when Lawrence made a poor and ill-advised lateral pass that Bubba Gernand intercepted. Baylor whirled down the field, mostly on passes, to TCU's 32-yard line. Four plays advanced the ball to the 24-yard line where TCU took it on downs, and the Green and Gold was through for the day.

Soon after the second quarter opened, TCU got possession on its own 40. A penalty pushed the Frogs back five and then they let fly.

On four plays they went 65 yards to a touchdown. The first 25 were on a forward pass and a lateral that went from Lawrence to Walls to a first down on the Baylor 27. Baugh faked a pass and ran 15 yards through the middle of the Baylor line. The climax play was a pass, Lawrence to Walls, who made a fine catch deep in the end zone. Roach kicked the extra point.

Lawrence intercepted a Baylor pass and ran it back 25 yards to Baylor's 34 to set the stage for the next score. On the first play from there, Baugh passed to Clark, racing north down the west sideline, for the six points. The play was the same one that TCU used to score two touchdowns against A&M. Clark caught the ball just back of Hal Finley on the 4-yard line and stepped over the goal line. Roach again converted.

The third quarter was all TCU's but the Frogs couldn't score, being stopped once on the 6-yard line.

A 48-yard march accounted for the third Christian score. It started after George Kline and Godwin recovered one of Russell's several fumbles. Kline cut through tackle on a reverse for 15 yards. Baugh added seven yards and Kline raced 11 to a first down on the four. A penalty pushed TCU back to the 9-yard line and from there, on the first play, Baugh passed to Needham who was open in the end zone. Manton converted the extra point.

A few minutes later Baugh intercepted a Baylor pass and made a fine 23-yard return to the Bears' 34. Four plays made 16 yards and a first down on the 18. Baugh made three and then again passed to Needham who was once more in the open behind the goal line. McCall converted twice. The first time TCU was off side and was penalized five yards and the next time there was nothing amiss.

When the game ended, TCU had the ball on the Baylor 45-yard line.

SCORE BY QUARTERS

TCU	0	14	0	14	—	28
Baylor	0	0	0	0	—	0

Frogs Overwhelm Longhorns

By Flem R. Hall

Fort Worth Star-Telegram

AUSTIN, Nov. 16, 1935

The all-victorious football forces of Texas Christian University roared on Saturday afternoon, walloping the University of Texas Longhorns, 28-0, in a game that convincingly demonstrated the Horned Frogs must be figured in national championship considerations.

Led by Slingin' Sam Baugh, who threw three touchdown passes, the Purple handled the Orange and White as it has not been handled this season. The margin of victory was greater than of either SMU or Rice over Texas, and it was piled up with startling ease. TCU reserves played the last third of the contest after the big lead had been established.

TCU scored one touchdown in the first quarter, another in the second and two in the first 10 minutes of the third. After that the Christians' second and third string more than held the Orange safe.

All the first three scores were made on passes thrown by Baugh. Willie Walls took the first on the 22-yard line and after tearing loose from two defenders, checked in back of the goal line. Walter Roach converted the extra point kick. He did the same after each of the other three touchdowns, too. All his place kicks were perfect.

Jimmy Lawrence made a beautiful running catch in the end zone for the next score. That play started on the Texas 12-yard line.

L.D. Meyer caught the 13-yard touchdown pass on the early minutes of the third quarter to put the Chris-

tians ahead, 21-0. He made a twisting leap in one corner of the south goal to make the shot good.

Tracy Kellow and Roach collaborated to manufacture the final touchdown. The guard blocked Bill Pitzer's punt and the end scooped it up and made a weaving run for 30 yards to cross the goal line.

Playing a much better defensive game than has been their usual custom, the Frogs smothered the vaunted Texas offense. After the first two minutes — when a fumble gave them a scoring chance — the Steers did not get within 25 yards of the TCU goal. All the Frog linemen turned in upended games but it was the guards, Kellow, Wilber (Cotton) Harrison and Glynn (Bull) Rogers who stood out.

Drew Ellis took complete charge of left tackle which has been so troublesome. Wilson Groseclose, Capt. Darrel Lester, Roach and Walls were perfect for the day.

Baugh was, of course, the back that overshadowed all others on both teams, but Jimmy Lawrence and Taldon Manton also did invaluable service. At times they carried the ball steadily down the field, and the Texas line was ripped to ribbons.

If the score and use of the reserves does not clearly reflect the Christians' superiority, consider the statistics: TCU made 17 first downs to Texas' five. The Frogs rolled up a net total of 355 yards gained on runs and passes to the Longhorns' 79 yards. Texas did not complete any of its 15 passes, four were intercepted.

Baugh makes his way through the Texas defense in TCU's 28-0 victory over the Longhorns.

TCU connected on only nine in 19 attempts but they were good for three touchdowns and a total of 215 yards.

The game was played before a crowd estimated at 12,000 and under conditions that would have been ideal for football if it had not been for a fresh north wind that swept the field lengthwise. As it was, the wind played little part in the play. The sun broke through the partly cloudy sky intermittently, but the temperature hovered around 50 degrees.

As is their habit, the Frogs got knocked back to their own goal line in the first minute. A fumble gave Texas the ball on the Purple 26-yard line, and Buster Jurecka and Irvin Gilbreath soon had a first down on the three-yard line. An offside penalty (the only one that TCU suffered throughout the afternoon) shoved the Frogs back to the one. Texas had three downs to make the yard. The Orange lost two on two attempts and then fumbled and lost the ball on third down.

Jurecka fumbled and Groseclose recovered. When Baugh punted out a cool 64 yards, Texas was through for the day.

A few minutes later, TCU got possession on its own 24 and from there they left fly with a 76-yard drive.

On the first pass, Baugh completed to George Kline for 31 yards and a first down on the Texas 45. Two plays failed. Baugh then passed to Walls deep over the middle and he ran 22 yards for a touchdown.

Walls made the catch while covered by two Steers, and managed to break loose. A beautiful block by Kline took out one of the two pursuers, and Walls beat the other to the goal line.

Shortly after the next kickoff (which Texas received), the quarter closed.

With the wind, Texas promptly punted to the TCU 31. TCU punted back and Texas launched a hard running attack from its own 30. It carried 25 yards before Pitzer was forced to punt. The kick was

Darrell Lester was an All-SWC and all-America center in 1934 and 1935.

over the goal and TCU's ball on its own 20. From there, TCU went 80 yards to score. Manton made 10 through the middle and Texas was penalized 15 for Arnold's roughing.

Baugh threw a long pass to Clark for 37 yards and a first down on the Texas 18. Clark was forced out of bounds by Van Zandt. A pass missed. Baugh faked a pass and ran six. He then passed to Lawrence in the end zone.

Early in the third quarter, TCU set sail from its own

35 to tally. The Purple first launched a running attack that swept down the field 37 yards to the Texas 28. Lawrence Manton and Baugh did the carrying.

Baugh then passed to Roach for eight yards. The next two runs failed. On the fourth-down pass, Collins interfered with Roach and Texas was penalized to that spot on the Longhorn 13. On the next play, Baugh passed to Meyer in the end zone for a touchdown. The little end made a fine catch. Roach again converted, and the score was TCU 21, Texas 0.

Shortly after the next kickoff Baugh returned a punt 35 yards to Texas' 25 and then threw a pass to Lawrence. Roach carried to the 10. Pitzer smashed the threat by intercepting a pass and returning it 41 yards to his 46. Harrison caught him from behind. Forced back to its 31, Texas tried to punt. Kellow blocked Pitzer's attempt. Roach scooped the ball up on the 31 and made a nice broken field run to the goal line. He also converted the point-after kick.

TCU substituted an entire new team, except for Lester. A few minutes later, a Frog fumble gave Texas the ball near the middle of the field. Tittle then replaced Lester.

Atchison raced 23 yards around right end for a first down on the TCU 29, the closest to pay dirt they had been since the first minutes of play. The third quarter closed with the ball there.

Tittle intercepted a pass to choke off the Texas bid. Montgomery punted 30 yards out on Texas' 40. McCall made 11 and fumbled when hit. Texas recovered on its 40. Neither side was able to gain with any consistency and a punting duel followed.

The TCU reserves finally made a first down running in their own end of the field. Montgomery followed up with a long pass to Blackmon who ran 18 yards for a total gain of 43 yards to a first down on the Texas 21. Four plays misfired and Texas took the ball on the 26. The game closed a minute later with Texas in possession in the middle of the field.

SCORE BY QUARTERS

TCU	7	7	14	0	—	28
Texas	0	0	0	0	—	0

Frogs Charge to Victory over Owls

By Flem R. Hall
Fort Worth Star-Telegram

FORT WORTH, Nov. 23, 1935

The flaming and furious Frogs of Texas Christian University, as audacious and clever a football battalion as ever stepped on a gridiron, put an end to all speculation to their prowess here on their own greensward Saturday afternoon by knocking the obstreperous Owls of Rice Institute into oblivion with a startling and smashing 27-6 score.

Paced by Slingin' Sam Baugh, Jarryin' Jimmy Lawrence, Capt. Darrell Lester, and with every man doing his part nobly, the Christians marked up their tenth victory of the season by handing the wise and tough old banjo-eyed Birds the worst defeat since they flew to a high place in the national ranking.

Baugh passed to three of the touchdowns and Lawrence ran the other one over.

The Christians started their storming assault to glory's peak by scoring in the first 20 seconds of play. Taking the opening kickoff, George Kline raced, behind beautiful blocking, 74 yards to the Rice 11-yard line. On the first play from scrimmage, Lawrence ran to his right, cut back and went over the goal standing up. Walter Roach converted.

Undismayed, the Owls swung back. Cutting loose all of their great running power, bound up in the legs of Bill Wallace, John McCauley and Buck Friedman, they ripped their way to a touchdown. Friedman made the last five yards of a 50-yard march. Baugh blocked John Sylvester's place-kick try for the extra point and the visitors from Houston were, for all practical purposes, through for the day.

The first quarter ended, 7 to 6, and as the teams exchanged goals. There was much concern in the TCU cheering section because the Frogs were losing the advantage of a stiff south wind that swept the field lengthwise. With startling suddenness, however, the white-shirted stalwarts revealed to the 20,000 spectators that instead of being through, they were just getting started. In quick succession they whipped over two touchdowns.

Taking the ball on its own 35, the TCU juggernaut tore 65 yards on nine plays. The first eight were running plays, featuring Lawrence, Rex Clark, Taldon Manton and Baugh. The ninth was a pass, Baugh to Lawrence, for a touchdown. That scoring play originated on the Rice 22 and Lawrence caught the ball while clear in the end zone. Roach again converted.

A few minutes later the home forces got possession on their own 20, and they covered 80 yards in six plays. Lawrence ripped off the first 16; Manton split the middle for the next 29 and then Clark raced 15 yards to a first down on the Owl 21.

After twice faking a pass and running to two three-yard gains. Baugh dropped back and cut loose a perfect shot that reached the uncovered L.D. Meyer deep in the end zone. Meyer gathered it in. Roach failed in his conversion effort.

The score was 20 to 6 when intermission rolled around.

Rice came back in the third quarter to launch a raging attack on the wings of a favorable wind. Twice Wallace led drives that reached the TCU 20, but it could go no further. The Frogs appeared content to sit back and play defensively. There was no scoring in the period.

As soon as the fourth quarter opened, the big Purple and White team came out of its shell and began pounding the enemy. Although they lost two apparent touchdowns, they succeeded in converting one, and when the final gun sounded, the reserves were attacking away inside the Rice 10-yard line. The final touchdown was made on an 11-yard pass. Baugh to Meyer, who was again loose in the end zone. The scoring play climaxed a swift 52-yard journey that required only three plays.

Baugh passed to Walter Roach for the first 32 yards and then to Clark for nine, before he rifled to Meyer. Roach didn't miss that time and the final score was spread on the minutes.

The statistics do not give an accurate picture of the game. Rice's 20 first downs to TCU's 17 and the Owls' total of 332 yards gained from scrimmage (runs and passes) to the Frogs 392 doesn't show the deadly ease with which the Christians shot the Birds down from long range.

The figures also do not take into account that TCU got ahead in the first seconds, stayed ahead all the way, and were content to let Rice gain out in the middle of the field while holding their own lead safe.

Wallace was the biggest ground gainer on the field making no less than 140 yards on 20 runs. Lawrence rolled up 74 yards in 13 attempts, an average of six yards to Wallace's seven.

Baugh was the boy who stopped the Owls from breaking the Southwest Conference tradition that champions never repeat. He completed 11 of the 19 passes he threw and they were good for more than 200 yards and three touchdowns.

SCORE BY QUARTERS

Rice	6	0	0	0	—	6
TCU	7	13	0	7	—	27

Dutch Meyers' Horned Frogs marched to a 12-1 record in 1936 and were named national champions.

SMU Defeats Frogs Before 36,000 Wild Fans

By Flem R. Hall
Fort Worth Star-Telegram

FORT WORTH, Nov. 30, 1935

In a game that sizzled and crackled with all the fierce fire of roaring Southwest football, the militant Mustangs of Southern Methodist University defeated a gallant Texas Christian University team, 20-14, here at newly expanded TCU Stadium as the second-greatest crowd (36,000) that ever saw a football game in Texas gasped at the bold, daring and audacious play of the two magnificent gridiron brigades.

With all the football world looking on or listening through the eyes and ears of a multitude of national critics and radio announcers, the Pony Express and the Horned Frogs put on a grand show — a typical, open free-scoring Southwest conflict — a game worthy of the position it held in national attention.

Although they threw only six passes, the Mustangs snatched victory out of the sunlit skies that canopied the perfect scene. With the score tied, 14-14, in the fourth quarter, with the ball on the TCU 37-yard line, Robert Finley, on fourth down with four yards to go for a first, flung a long, true pass straight down the east sideline toward the north goal. Rambling Robert Wilson evaded the defensive left halfback (Harold McClure) and made a marvelous catch on about the 4-yard line and, recovering from a stumble, crossed the goal line for the winning six points.

Starting the conflict as sharp as tacks, the Ponies whipped over a touchdown in the first four minutes of play and added another seven points in the early part of the second quarter. The dauntless Christians fought back with fierce and deadly effectiveness. They scored once before the half, and tied the count, 14-all, in the early minutes of the fourth quarter.

SMU gave a clear impression that it was the better team for the day and deserved to win by receiving the next kickoff and scoring without losing possession. Maurice Orr, who converted after the first two touchdowns, failed in his third attempt and hope still burned brightly in the breasts of TCU supporters. And not without reasons. Twice within the remaining six minutes the white-shirted force swept into threatening position. They were stopped once on the SMU 28-yard line, and the final gun found them completing pass after pass that had carried them to the Methodist 35.

The Blue and Red played without the services of its star fullback, Harry Shuford, but TCU lost Rex Clark, an ace left halfback, on the second play of the game and lost only after Jarrin' Jimmy Lawrence, who scored both touchdowns, was forced from the game by injuries.

No. 27 was Finley, the substitute back who threw the deciding touchdown pass, the 185-pounder from Corsicana, who whipped another tremendous pass (33 yards) that set the stage for a nine-yard touchdown gallop by Wilson (No. 11), who played a full 60 minutes of brilliant football. No. 23 was Maco Stewart, who caught the

Jimmy Lawrence (8), who scored two touchdowns for TCU, races up field for big yardage.

first Finley pass and rounded out a fine afternoon with a sweet game at end. No. 47 was Truman Spain, who proved his all-America worth by playing the finest game at tackle seen here this season.

No. 20 was Shelley Burt, the rugged right halfback, who bowled his way through the TCU line for 51 yards in 11 attempts. No. 21 was Bill Tipton, the left end, who twice helped the Blue and Red out of trouble. He made the first touchdown possible by recovering a Wilson fumble for a seven-yard gain on the TCU 13-yard line.

No. 45, 8 and 22 for TCU were Sam Baugh, Jimmy Lawrence and Darrel Lester, respectively. Slingin' Sam, shooting with all his accuracy, completed 17 of 44 passes and would have a much better average if his usually sure-handed receivers had been catching the ball as well as they ordinarily do. Time after time he laid the ball on the right spot, against the best defense TCU has opposed,

only to have his receivers muff the passes.

Baugh accounted for 180 yards of ground gaining on passes. He punted magnificently, averaging 48 yards from the line of scrimmage and he did as swell a job of running and on defense.

SMU marched 73 yards in the first four minutes for its first touchdown. Starting from their own 27, the Mustangs ripped 19 yards on running plays, with Burt doing most of the damage. Then Burt passed to Sprague. Finley led another running assault that made a first down on the 20. Then Wilson fumbled on an end sweep and Tipton recovered on the TCU 13.

Burt burst through for a first down on the 1-yard line and Finley carried it over in one try. Orr converted.

The next scoring jaunt traveled 80 yards on just five plays. Wilson started it with a 22-yard jaunt around TCU's left end. Burt got three yards at tackle, and Finley broke through for a first down on the Frog 42. Burt made a yard, and then Finley shot a long pass over George Kline to Stewart, who made an unbelievable catch on the TCU nine-yard line. On the next play Wilson again swept left end, and this time for a touchdown, just beating defenders to the northeast corner. Orr again converted.

Just before that swift flight, TCU had made a 74-yard drive only to be stopped on the SMU 16.

A great punt by Baugh, one that sailed 50 yards and out of bounds on the SMU four, started the first successful bid for points. The punt was only to the Mustang 26. From there TCU went to the five. A penalty against Sprague for interfering with a pass receiver gave TCU a first down on the 2-yard line, and from there Lawrence drove over. Roach converted, which made it 14-7, and the half ended.

The third period was scoreless but the teams battled madly between the 30-yard lines, and the play was marked by teeth-rattling tackles and brutal blocking. Just before the period closed, Walter Roach intercepted a Mustang pass on the TCU 44 and Baugh passed to Lawrence for a first down on SMU's 43.

On the first play of the final quarter, Baugh again tossed a short pass to Lawrence, who tore off a 17-yard gain. Two plays later, Baugh passed to Willie Walls for a first down on the Pony eight.

Two passes failed to click, but on the third Lawrence made the big catch and went over. It was on that play that he was hurt and had to retire. Roach converted to knot the score.

Then came the winning assault.

Roach's kickoff was short and J. R. Smith, who was the star of the remainder of the game, returned to his own 47. Two plays made a first down on the Frog 43. When the next three plays netted only six yards, it appeared that the Ponies would have to kick. But, gambling boldly for victory, Finley passed instead and it worked — and put SMU in the Rose Bowl.

SCORE BY QUARTERS

SMU	7	7	0	6	—	20
TCU	0	7	0	7	—	14

Notable Sports Writers Honored at Worth Hotel

Visiting sports writers gathering here from throughout the nation to cover the TCU-SMU championship game Saturday afternoon for their respective newspapers were guests of the Fort Worth Chamber of Commerce at an informal dinner at The Worth Hotel on Friday evening. There were no speeches, only food and other entertainment for the visitors.

Coaches of the rival teams attended the dinner and mingled with the numerous sports writers who taxed the press box at TCU to more than its capacity of 100 persons.

New names are being added to the list daily and it now includes such well known sports writers as Grantland Rice, Paul Gallico, New York News; Joe Williams, New York World-Telegram; Bill Cunningham, Boston Post; Maxwell Stiles, Los Angeles Herald-Examiner; Dick Cullum, Minneapolis Twin-Journal; Bus Ham, Oklahoma City Daily Oklahoman; B. A. Bridgewater, Tulsa World; Bill Parker, Associated Press; Jack O'Brien, San Antonio Evening News; Jinx Tucker, Waco News-Tribune; Dick Baldwin, United Press; Dick Freeman, Houston Chronicle; Jere Hayes, Dallas Times-Herald; George White, The Dallas Morning News; Lloyd Gregory, Houston Post; Millard Cope, Sweetwater; Collier Parris, Lubbock; Max Bentley, Abilene, and others.

Baugh's Aim Is True as Frogs Beat Santa Clara

By Flem R. Hall

Fort Worth Star-Telegram

SAN FRANCISCO, Dec. 7, 1935

By striking suddenly at the start of the game and again as the second half opened, TCU defeated Santa Clara University, 10-6, here Saturday afternoon in a game that gave the 25,000 spectators a fair sample of the kind of football played in the Southwest.

It was place kicks that gave the Christians their four-point margin. Walter Roach's successful boot following the touchdown in the first minute of play, and Taldon Manton's 33-yard field goal in the early part of the third quarter were the difference.

Playing without the services of Jimmy Lawrence and Rex Clark, who were in civilian clothes on the bench, the Texans took advantage of a break on the second play of the game to go ahead and Manton's perfect kick gave the Frogs a 10-point lead.

The game was rocking along quietly until late in the third period when the Broncos turned a TCU fumble into a 77-yard touchdown play. Fullback

Baugh, who completed 14 of 28 passes against Santa Clara, lets loose a bomb on the Broncos' defense.

127

Falascht failed to convert, but the six points had put Santa Clara back in the ball game and from then until the final gun the play took on extra sparkle and ruggedness.

TCU, however, kept complete charge of the situation. While keeping the Broncos bottled up in their own end of the field, the Purple twice drove into striking distance only to be stopped by a team that refused to quit. Instead of trying to protect its slender lead by playing a safe and sane running game, TCU kept right on passing in the fourth quarter, even in its own end of the field. On the next-to-last play of the game, Sullivan of Santa Clara intercepted a pass on his own 12-yard line. The charging Texas line smothered the next play for an eight-yard loss, and the game closed with Santa Clara in possession on its own four.

The first kickoff by Santa Clara was over the goal line and TCU took the ball on its 20. On the first play, Sam Baugh quick-kicked far over the safetyman's head and it rolled to the five-yard line. When the safety, Seramin, finally caught up with the ball he fumbled and Drew Ellis, who had come down the field fast, recovered on the four-yard line.

The first TCU play, a plunge, lost a yard. Then Baugh passed neatly to Harold McClure in the end zone for the six points. The pass was a short one over the right side of the line, and McClure, playing in the place of Lawrence, made the catch in the clear near the east side line, back of the north goal. Walter Roach's kick was high and true.

There was no more scoring in the first two quarters. TCU kept trying but made mistakes that prevented any sustained drives. Santa Clara, on the other hand, was unable to cash in on its attempt to steal the show with TCU's favorite mode of attack — passing. The Broncos completed several and twice advanced within 30 yards of the scoring station, but when backed to their own 24. The TCU line, which wasn't impressive in the middle of the field, threw Santa Clara plays for repeated losses.

TCU again received the kickoff at the start of the second half. George Kline fumbled the oval on his four but picked it up and raced through a big hole to the left to reach the Santa Clara 40 before he was knocked over the east side line. Manton drove through the middle for 10 yards of the first play and 12 on the second. Baugh passed to L.D. Meyer for a first down on the Broncos' 14. One running play lost a yard and two passes failed.

On fourth down, Manton dropped-kicked back to the 23-yard line and with Baugh holding, place-kicked squarely between the uprights and over the bar for the three points that made the score 10-0.

The Frogs were marching when a play exploded in their faces to give Santa Clara six points and new life. They were on the 24-yard line when Vic Montgomery fumbled as he hit the line on a reverse to the left. The ball shot into the arms of Dutton, the Santa Clara end, who was moving in the opposite direction. Dutton broke into the clear and raced 41 yards to the TCU 15 before he was overhauled by Kline. As he was tackled, Dutton made a smart and pretty lateral to Dowd, who scampered the remaining 35 yards unhampered across the goal. Falascht's kick was low and wide.

Before and after that play, Santa Clara never threatened seriously. In the fourth quarter it was just a question of whether the Broncos would get another scoring break, or if they'd be able to hold the TCU attack. They succeeded in the latter but never had a chance to win the game.

Montgomery, who played most of the game in Lawrence's place after McClure was removed because he made poorly advised and costly lateral passes that failed, more than made up for his one error by intercepting two passes and playing a generally fine game.

TCU won the game in the book keeping department as well as on the scoreboard. The Frogs made 14 first downs, all earned, to Santa Clara's seven earned and one on a penalty. The total net yards gained were 206 to 127 in favor of the White Shirted invaders. On running plays, TCU gained 111 yards to Santa Clara's 109, and on passes the totals were TCU 124, Santa Clara 61. Baugh averaged 42 yards on his 12 punts to 33 for Santa Clara kickers.

The Christians put on the passing show that was expected of them in spite of the fact that Broncos'

coach Clipper Smith used a special defense to stop that form of attack. Baugh tossed 28 of the 29 TCU forwards and completed 14 of them for an even .500 average. Three were intercepted and the others fell incomplete. Kline dropped one in his hands over the goal line, but it didn't matter because the Frogs were offside on the play anyway.

After the game hundreds of fans swarmed on the field and mobbed the slinger from Sweetwater with congratulations and for his autograph.

Local observers credited Santa Clara with playing its best game of the season, and that was partly due to the fact that several stars who have been out most of the year with injuries returned to service.

SCORE BY QUARTERS

TCU	7	0	3	0	—	10
Santa Clara	0	0	6	0	—	6

Horned Frogs Outduel LSU in Sugar Bowl

By *Flem R. Hall*
Fort Worth Star-Telegram

NEW ORLEANS, Jan. 1, 1936

Playing as glorious a game as ever a Texas Christian University team turned in, the purple-clad football Horned Frogs defeated the Terrible Tigers of Louisiana State University, champions of the Southeastern Conference, 3-2, here this New Year's afternoon in the second annual feature of the Sugar Bowl's midwinter Sports Carnival.

An astounding 36-yard field goal by fullback Taldon Manton won the ball game, which was played under conditions that were about as bad as possible.

Dark and cold from the start, the afternoon turned rainy at the half, and the gridiron was a veritable morass before the end. Heavy rains on Saturday, Tuesday and Wednesday morning had the gridiron soggy and slippery before the first kickoff, and it became steadily worse as the play progressed. A cold wind out of the Northeast swept the rain in slanting sheets diagonally across the field.

It was the consensus of the press box after the game

TCU's stubborn defense stops the attempted touchdown dive of LSU's Bill Crass at the 1-yard line.

130

SUGAR BOWL CLASSIC JAN. 1, 1936
Crass Misses Touchdown by Inches in Third Quarter

that the better team won, that TCU out-gamed the Tigers, who started the game as an 8-to-5 favorite; out-fought, outthought and outplayed the Bengals from Baton Rouge, to gain the narrow-margined victory.

In spite of the terrible weather the game was witnessed by approximately 37,000 fans, who occupied nearly every available seat in Tulane Stadium to form the largest crowd ever to witness a sporting event in the Deep South. And the customers stuck right down to the last play. So intense was the interest in the desperate play that discomfort was disregarded until the timekeeper's clock stopped the fray with TCU in possession of the ball on the LSU 23-yard line.

All points of the ball game were scored in the second quarter. LSU got two on an automatic safety to draw first blood, and then the Frogs, stung into action, whipped up three points within two minutes.

The safety was called after Sam Baugh, the No. 1 player of the game, accidentally stepped over his own end zone line while trying to launch a pass. He was rushed hard by Paul Carroll, the Tigers' right tackle, and managed to get the ball off only after he had retreated a step too far, and an alert official called automatic scoring foul.

The ball was put in play for a free kick from the 29-yard line. Walter Roach got off a long kickoff to the LSU 40-yard line. On the first play from there Bill Crass fumbled, and Willie Walls, who played a marvelous game, recovered for TCU. Jimmy Lawrence, who played most of the game brilliantly in spite of a severe leg injury, passed to Walls for a first down on the 16-yard line.

The next three plays netted a three-yard loss, but left the ball only about 10 yards from the middle of the field. Center Jack Tittle passed the wet, slick, heavy ball back perfectly to Baugh, who set it down on the 26-yard line. Manton drove his right toe into the ball and it took off like a perfect golf approach shot and sailed squarely be-

---

Tillie Manton booted the game-winning field goal, which defeated LSU in the 1936 Sugar Bowl.

tween the uprights and well over the cross bar for what proved to be the ball game.

It was the third time in as many meetings that place-kicked field goals have figured vitally in TCU-LSU football games. In 1931 the Frogs defeated the Tigers, 3-0, and the following season they tied, 3-3. Today's game was the third gridiron contest between the two.

No more spectacular and engrossing football was ever

played under such adverse conditions as existed here. Ordinarily mud battles are dull shoving contests, but that was not the case in this Sugar Bowl scrap. Both teams tried everything in the book.

There were three hair-raising goal-line stands — two by TCU and one by LSU; there was plenty of passing, especially by LSU; as sensational punting a game as was ever produced, a half dozen long and dazzling runs; daring and gambling play, and a field goal that'll go down in football history as one of the finest.

TCU played most of the game minus the services of three of its brightest stars — left halfback George Kline, all-American center Darrell Lester and halfback Rex Clark. Kline went out early in the first quarter, never to return, on account of his peculiar eye trouble. Lester suffered an injured right arm stopping a crashing plunge by Bill Crass on the goal line in the second quarter and had to leave the game, not to return. Clark played only one down and that was only by the courtesy of TCU coaches Meyer and Wolf, who wanted the injured senior star to be able to say he played in the 1936 Sugar Bowl game.

Sophomore Bob Harrell played most of the time in place of injured Kline and gave a good account of him-

self. Another sophomore, Jack Tittle, filled in for Lester and delivered an outstanding performance. So brilliant was he that the Frogs did not miss their captain. Tittle passed the ball back accurately all afternoon, blocked well on offense, stopped all LSU plays that came his way and batted down two passes.

Gaynell Tinsely, LSU's all-American left end, was all of that on defense, but just so-so on offense. Abe Mickal, Rock Reed, Crass and Jess Fatheree took turns in turning loose their versatile skill at the embattled Christians, and, although they flashed time and time again, they could never put together enough consecutive plays to cross the valiantly defended TCU goal line.

Tracy Kellow, Wilson Groseclose, Drew Ellis, Glynn Rogers, Walls, Tittle and Walter Roach saw to that. Those linemen were given invaluable help by Manton, who just about proved himself the finest fullback in the South, backing up the TCU line so well that the Tigers were prevented from scoring a touchdown for the only time during the long season. He also distinguished himself by his sure-handed work on holding the ball on the intricate reverses and spinners that the Frogs persisted in using with success in spite of the treacherous slipperiness of the leather.

Jimmy Lawrence gave a great demonstration of determination and courage by playing most of the game despite his bad ankle. He did not just stand out there; he played as well as any back on the field, except one. That one exception was Sam Baugh — that junior quarterback — did the greatest job of punting this old field ever saw, and not one of the scores of veteran football observers who saw the game could recall a contest that produced kicking to compare with it.

LSU had three really fine punters in Mickal, Crass and Fatheree, and they each did marvelous work; but Baugh outlasted and outkicked them all. Not only that; he made the longest run of the day — a 44-yard gallop off tackle that just lacked two yards of scoring a touchdown in the final minutes of the game. It was the run that made the one-point margin safe in the last three minutes.

SCORE BY QUARTERS

TCU	0	3	0	0	—	3
LSU	0	2	0	0	—	2

Texas Fans Cheer as Frogs Triumph

By Amos Melton
Fort Worth Star-Telegram

Wet, exhausted, but entirely happy, the thousands of Texas grid fans who cheered the TCU Horned Frogs to victory in the Sugar Bowl game Wednesday afternoon surged out of the Tulane Stadium to stage a mighty celebration in the downtown hotels and streets. Cheering, singing visitors from the Lone Star State paraded the streets in exultation amid the carnival and no less enthusiastic shouts of the Louisianians. They staged a fitting triumph in honor of the great Frog machine that whipped the LSU Tigers here today.

Arriving early at the game, the thousands of Texans sat during the battle despite a cold, steady rain that fell throughout the last half. Not until the Frogs, tired but victorious, gathered in front of the Texas section for happy reunion with their "folks" while the purple band played the Alma Mater, did any Texan think of quitting the field. Fans and players stood in the rain to hug each other in glee.

So busy were the visitors with their celebration that many were pushed to catch the first returning TCU-Star-Telegram special train that departed at 8 o'clock. A second special followed a few minutes later. Both trains echoed with the happy shouts of the Frog fans. The specials are due to arrive in Fort Worth at 10 a.m. Thursday.

The press box, extending for some 50 yards along the top of the west stand, was packed and jammed with writers from all sections of the country. Almost every leading city in the Old South was represented, as well as the Texas cities of Fort Worth, Houston, Beaumont and several others. Four radio booths were scenes of busy activity. Cy Leland of WBAP, The Star-Telegram station, was at the mike for the National Broadcasting Company, which listed more than 80 stations on the hookup.

Frog Bombers Triumph over Porkers!

By Ed Prell
Fort Worth Star-Telegram

FORT WORTH, Oct. 3, 1936

"Put me in there at quarterback, Coach, and I'll play you a game of football," was the earnest plea of Sam Baugh in the dressing room yesterday afternoon before they went out on the TCU greensward to tie into Arkansas' tall, red-clad giants. Well, suh, Sammy Baugh played Coach "Dutch" Meyer a game of football as the Frogs, the Porkers and 9,000 fans will testify.

At the finish of a game that saw 71 aerials flipped into the warm afternoon air, the Frogs carried an 18-14 lead, eloquent testimony to the gridiron world that they will carry their famous punch of 1935.

The luck of the draw, and not any last-minute change on the little Dutchman's part, put the Sweetwater slinger in the pilot's slot. It was O'Brien at quarterback if the Frogs received, or Baugh if they kicked. They kicked, and Baugh never gave Meyer a chance to give little "Dallas Davey" the warm-up sign.

In fact, as the minutes wore on, some of the more dubious were beginning to wonder if Davey O'Brien weren't a myth. But there was nothing mythical about Baugh. He was all-American to a "T" all the way, as he heaved the ball, slammed into those crouched red-shirts, or booted the ball far down the field.

Keyed to a fighting pitch by Meyer's driving tactics and threats of drastic changes, and playing on a dry field bathed with an Indian summer sun, the Frogs looked for a throwback to last year's powerful club.

They mixed Baugh's bullet-like passes with a varied running attack and the latter was the big surprise. The forwards opened up gaping holes, especially in the center of the line. The running star turned out to be Donkey Roberts of Fort Worth, the string-bean, 170-pound fullback who averaged six yards in 14 blasts at the enemy line.

First to score on a 56-yard march that began when Willie Walls, the Arkansas boy playing end, recovered a fumble and the Frogs, nevertheless, trailed 7-6 at halftime. But they started from their own 42 early in the third period to a score and then added one in the final period. The Porkers, still desperately trying, managed to land their second touchdown with two minutes left, but the Frogs froze the ball the remainder of the time.

When all the tabulation was checked and rechecked, it revealed the Frogs had amassed 19 first downs to 14 for the boys from the tall pine country, which oddly enough was just one point off the final score.

As for the passes, they added up 30 for the Frogs and 41 for the Porkers, but this is easily explained. Many of the enemy heaves were born of sheer desperation, coming as they did when TCU was out in front. The yardage on the passes was 228 for the Hogs against 183 for the Frogs.

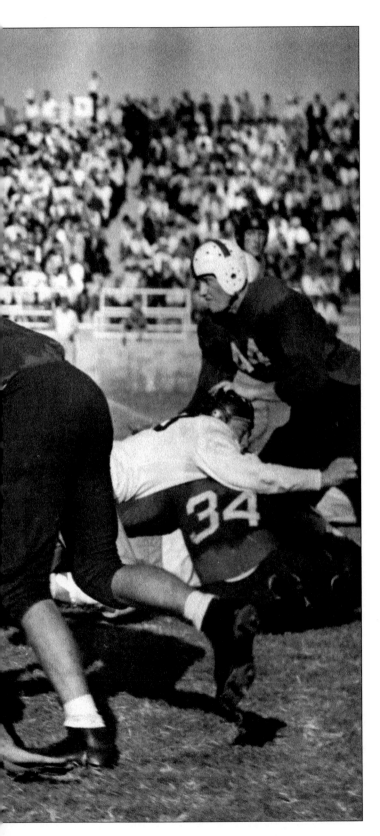

Baugh was in there for 60 minutes. So were Red Dog Clifford and Vic Montgomery. War Wilkinson, who started at fullback, gave way to the surprising Roberts, who sparkled both on offense and defense.

As it was the only game played in the Southwest Conference to date, the Frogs jumped into undisputed possession of the lead. It was their ninth victory, and second straight over the Porkers.

There was a murmur from the sun-baked crowd when Baugh was announced at quarterback, but this was just the first of a large afternoon of surprises.

No sooner had the Porkers received Walter Roach's thudding kick than they started filling the air with leather, but the Frogs held after one pass clicked. The first of Baugh's potent passes was one to Clifford, who tore down the west side line to the Frogs' six, a gain of 14 yards, but the drive came to an abrupt end when Monty fumbled and Lunday recovering.

But on the next play Walls, who perhaps will be expatriated by his home state for his busy afternoon, scooped up a loose ball dropped by Holt on the Porkers 44, and from this spot the Frogs battered their way to the opening score.

It was Baugh to Roach and Baugh to Walls for seven yards each and the Porkers quickly took time out. Over the goal line zoomed another Baugh shot, and Clifford just missed reaching it.

Then Baugh clicked with a six-yarder to Montgomery and proceeded to cross up the Hogs by plowing left tackle for six and another first down. Then a pass to Montgomery for 14 yards to the 5.

Over the goal again winged the ball, but no one was there. Baugh faded back and the anxious Hogs started covering the receivers. But Wilkinson took the pass-back and smashed over center.

Roach's place kick was off the mark.

Soon afterward, the Hogs made their initial first down and then they clicked three more in succession at the 11, with Robbins throwing and Benton receiving for the biggest gains.

Baugh, noticing a wide opening in the Arkansas defense, rambles upfield.

Then an eight-yard flip from Robbins to Rawlings and the Frogs were backed to their 3.

The Frogs held twice, then Rawlings dropped a sure touchdown pass along the west side line. But the same play, on fourth down, worked and Rawlings shot over, just getting past the little red flag in the corner.

Owen came in and kicked the extra point to make it 7-6. Walls took the kickoff and breezed back to the Arkansas 45, where Benton slapped him down just when it appeared he might be away. Then the quarter ended.

Wilkinson and Montgomery tried line-smashing for a chance, but the drive stopped when Baugh's pass over the goal line was incomplete. The Porkers came back fighting. Sloan, who had replaced Robbins, threw a beauty to Benton and he lateraled to Martin for 23 yards. Sloan then flipped to Hamilton, another newcoming end, and this one was 14 yards to take the ball into Frog territory, at the 36.

This is where Roberts came into the battle. A Sloan pass spurted off Martin's outstretched hands and Montgomery snatched it and was brought down on the TCU 12. Baugh and Roberts made it a first down, but the Frogs were put in a hole when Baugh's punt was blocked. Clifford was on it like a rabbit on the 11, and Baugh booted out on his own 30.

Arkansas' persistent pass attack was topped when Roberts deflected Rawlings' toss to Clifford, who brought it back to the Frogs' 34 and Roberts, in two thrusts, made it first down on the 44. Baugh and Montgomery bumped the line for another first down, and Baugh passed to Montgomery, who was chased out of bounds on the Hogs' 23. The line-crashing continued with Clifford skirting left end and on a reverse for six and the surprising Roberts bulling through the middle for seven to the 10.

On fourth down, Rawlings intercepted Baugh's pass, back of the goal line, and threaded back to the 28, lateraling to Brown, who finally was hauled down on the Porkers' 35.

Another lateral advanced it 13 yards as the half closed.

Before the half was very old, the Frogs had gone ahead again, this time for good. From their own 42, the Frogs kept plugging until they had passed the final chalk line.

Roberts and Clifford bucked for a first down, and Baugh followed up with a pass to Roach on the Arkansas 37, with Roberts getting the necessary yardage for first down on a plunge.

Another heave to Roach netted 12 yards and then Baugh churned over left tackle for three yards. Then, on a spinner, Roberts raced through a gaping hole at left guard for the touchdown, a 21-yard run.

Montgomery had no better luck kicking for the extra point, with Gilmore blocking it.

A little later, Clifford almost got away on a reverse around left end. Keen finally hauling him down after a 11-yard gain. Roberts fumbled; recovered by Benton. Even though ahead, the Frogs refused to play safe football. When they got the ball again on their 30, Baugh flipped a 16-yard pass to Montgomery. Then he kicked out on the enemy five.

Robbins, back of his goal line showed plenty of spunk in passing, and the effort was good for a 13-yard gain. As the third quarter ended, Baugh intercepted a pass on the Hogs' 42.

The Frogs started clicking from midfield early in the final quarter when Baugh took Holt's punt on the run and slithered down the west side line, being felled heavily on the six. Baugh's shoulder was injured, but he recovered after a time out. They couldn't make it, and the Hogs took the ball on their 20.

A lateral, Holt to Benton to Sloan, brought the ball up to the TCU 45, but the tide turned again when Walls recovered another fumble, this one by Sloan on the Arkansas 37. Baugh and Roberts teamed for a first down on plunges. Then, after two short gains, Baugh passed to Montgomery in the flat and he romped over for a 22-yard touchdown play. Roach again missed.

The Porkers, rising up again, started a steady touchdown drive from their 35, with Robbins' passes showing the way. A fourth-down flip to Benton was good for a first down on the Frogs' 10. And on third down, Benton in a kneeling position just over the goal line, gathered in Robbins' sizzling throw. Owens kicked goal.

That was the last display of fireworks. The Frogs took the kickoff.

SCORE BY QUARTERS

Arkansas	7	0	0	7	—	14
TCU	6	6	0	6	—	18

Frogs Crush Texas

By Ed Prell
Fort Worth Star-Telegram

FORT WORTH, Nov. 7, 1936

When a football team wins a game in the southwest Conference in the first quarter, it's good. When it does the same thing twice, you furnish the adjectives.

That's your Texas Christian University eleven that this morning looms a favorite for the first time in this topsy-turvy race.

The Frogs, with rejuvenated Sam Baugh at the controls, bewildered the hapless University of Texas Longhorns with a fearful passing and running attack yesterday afternoon, 27-6, to the complete satisfaction of 15,000 homecoming fans, who didn't mind the chill air or the occasional splotches of rain.

It was a ridiculously easy triumph over a team that although often beaten, had played Southern Methodist, Rice and Baylor close games.

The Frogs' advance in the conference race was not confined to their own gridiron. With Texas A&M scoring a stunning upset

Davey O'Brien, the backup to Baugh at quarterback, earned all-America honors in 1938.

over the Southern Methodist University Mustangs, TCU bounced into a first place tie with the rangy Arkansas Porkers, who subdued Rice at Fayetteville.

The Longhorns, prepared for a devastating aerial attack from the great Baugh in the first quarter, were caught unprepared by the Frogs' strongest running attack of the season. When the route was all over, Hal McClure, the substitute right halfback for the injured Johnny Hall, had rung up each of the four touchdowns, all on off-tackle slashes.

Baugh's passing, instead of directly account for the scoring, served to move the ball into scoring position, mixed in as they were with quick, darting stabs at the lips by Scott McCall, Donkey Roberts, McClure and even Baugh himself.

The game followed almost the same pattern as the Baylor route of the previous Saturday. It was boom-boom and two touchdowns in the first quarter. The Frogs took up the warfare again and scored for the third time midway in the second quarter.

That was the signal for Baugh and several other regulars to stream for the bench, while the shock troops took charge. But they didn't do so good, although with Davey O'Brien in there the Frogs retained their 20-0 advantage at halftime.

The reserves though held their own at the outset and it appeared as though the scoring was over for the day. TCU was playing a careful game, trying out its running plays and taking no chances whatever.

But suddenly, with half of the third quarter gone, the Longhorns came to life with Hugh (Big Bad) Wolfe leading the assault. They were delayed twice by penalties on their excursion toward the goal line, but finally put it over, then missed the kick for the extra point.

This was with less than a minute to play in the quarter, but Coach Dutch Meyer, fearful that the big Austin team would get out of control, rushed his starters back into action.

They put an end to all the foolishness and with Baugh manning the Frogs again, they marched up the field for a touchdown from their 17-yard line to put on the last scoring flourish of a wide open and rough battle.

In this, their most notable offensive showing of the season, the Frogs registered 24 first downs, all but three coming from their own efforts.

They rang the ball on running plays 12 times and registered nine more firsts by passing. The other three came on Texas penalties, of which there were seven for 85 yards, the violations being for such assorted gridiron crimes as off-side, holding, clipping and roughing, not to mention an interference that helped the Frogs spring their first touchdown.

Baugh completed nine out of 11 passes in the first and second quarters during the spectacular scoring surge. Then, after throwing off his storm coat when Texas threatened, Baugh wound up completing

five more passes out of eight. This gave him 14 completions in 19 tries for 127 yards.

The old Masonic Home backfield trio of McClure, McCall and Roberts, playing together for the first time since their high school games, all turned in strong performances. So did Bob Harrell.

Baugh capped his fine passing show with a 61-yard run on a pass interception late in the game. He was hauled down on the seven-yard line and the Frogs were pounding away with another touchdown in sight when hostilities ceased.

The Frogs' first touchdown on an interrupted drive

Ki Aldrich was a three-time All-SWC center in 1936-38 and an all-America in 1938.

from their own 23, with every man in the backfield carrying the ball, on spinners and reverses. Roberts made the big gains with thrusts over center for 18 and 10 yards. Baugh, trying to plunge over from the one-foot line, fumbled, but Roberts recovered and McClure smashed over right tackle for touchdown No. 1.

The rain was coming down now and there was a rush for newspapers to use as umbrellas. One play after taking the kickoff, Texas fumbled, Sheridan being the offender, with Willie Walls pouncing on the ball 16 yards from the pay station.

Baugh's first pass to McCall was broken up by Lawson over the goal line. Then Baugh fired a shovel heave to McClure for five yards and another to McClure that put the ball on the four-yard line for first down.

Roberts gained a yard on a spinner, then McClure knifed over right tackle to really get started on his touchdown spree. Capt. Wally Roach, whose first kick for the extra point had been blocked by Clint Small, the Texas captain, made his second attempt good to put the Frogs out in front by 13 points, the touchdown being made shortly before the first quarter closed.

Early in the next period, the Frogs on their 26, as the result of a punt exchange, were fined 15 for clipping and Baugh punted out with the Longhorns coming back to the TCU 40. Texas couldn't get anywhere, though but it was still worse, from the Longhorn standpoint, when Roberts leaped into the air, hauled down Jud Atchison's pass and galloped 19 yards to put the ball on the enemy 38. This play set up the third touchdown drive, with Baugh beginning another air barrage. Harrell took his long pass in the flat for two yards, stumbling as he caught it. Then McClure took one for 14 yards and Harrell speared a shovel pass, threading his way for nine yards to the Texas 14. Roberts made it a first down on a four-yard plunge and on a reverse McClure sped around the Longhorn right side for the score. Roach again kicked the extra point.

It was here that Meyer gave his veteran a rest, and the remainder of the period was hum-drum in the light of what had happened before. Texas' offensive was stepped up a bit as the second half opened, but a penalty always cropped up when the Austin boys really started clicking. From their 28 they started to worry the Frogs. Atchi-

son and Wolfe plunged for a first down. Then Atchison was penalized 15 yards for holding and on the very next play assessed the same yardage for illegal use of the hands.

An interception of O'Brien's pass by Peterson on the Longhorn's 48 was the signal for a new drive. Atchison opened up with passes, two straight ones putting the ball on the Frogs 23, but the Steers drew a 15-yard fine for holding and O'Brien stopped the threat by a fine leaping interception of Atchison's pass on his 18.

Back came the Steers, this time from midfield after a punting party. Atchison passed to Arnold, who lateraled to Small for a 20-yard gain. By this time, the regular TCU ends were back in the combat. Then Atchison unfurled a long one to Peterson, who lateraled on the 20 to Wolfe just as he was bout to be tackled. The burly fullback gave a neat exhibition of broken field running, skidding over the goal line with a pack of Frogs charging in his wage. Wolfe missed the place kick for extra point.

More Frog regulars came back after this show of Texas power. The Longhorns kept up their dizzy passing, but lost the ball on downs on the Purple 34. McClure fumbled after catching a Baugh pass and Launey recovered on the TCU 42. Wolfe slashed around right end for 19 yards, but three Frogs broke through them and spilled Atchison for a 7-yard loss. Wolfe crashed through again and lateraled to Atchison to put the ball on the 19, then on the next play fumbled, with Harrell recovering on the 17.

Next, Baugh engineered the final touchdown parade. He passed to Walls for 11 yards and Harrell drove off tackle for seven more with Roberts getting enough yardage for a first down. A pass to Harrell took the ball to the Texas 32 where Harrell was chased out of bounds. Then a 12-yard heave to Roach, who ran to the 9-yard line. Roach, who fumbled, was kneed by Small; and the ensuing penalty put the ball on the 1-yard line. Roberts took it to the one-foot line, McClure dived over left tackle to can the biggest individual scoring exhibition in the conference of the season. Roach's toe worked again.

SCORE BY QUARTERS

Texas	0	0	6	0	—	6
TCU	13	7	0	7	—	27

Baugh's Passing Topples Undefeated Broncos

By Amos Melton

Fort Worth Star-Telegram

SAN FRANCISCO, Dec. 12, 1936

Those TCU Horned Frogs, God bless 'em, are the fightenist, guttiest, most magnificent gang of football players that ever came down any pike.

Fort Worth has always been proud of that Purple squad. But all of Texas and the southwest would have swelled with pride to see their own boys batter into defeat the last untied and undefeated major team in the nation here Saturday afternoon in Santa Clara, by 9-0.

Yes sir, the Texans had a good reputation, they had a great team and they were all fine folks, but defeat the mighty Santa Clara Broncos?

TCU couldn't win. The sport writers all said so, the coaches over this section were certain of the game and the California fans had only pity for the boys from Texas.

Well, those fightin' battling, rootin'-tootin' boys from the cow country gave 40,000 bugs in Kezar Stadium the jolt of their lives. They not only won, but decisively. The score might have been bigger had the Purple not been content to sit back and hold its safe lead in the final chapter.

Walter Roach snagged Baugh's pass for the game's only touchdown.

Just get this picture. Hundreds of miles from home, down on the floor of a mammoth stadium, before 80,000 hostile eyes, against the hardest hitting club they've played all season, the white-shirted boys might well have folded. But they didn't come out here to get licked, and so they didn't.

For the first few minutes, the little band of Frog supporters had a sinking feeling. The Broncos started right off with a deceptive flanker play that caught Capt. Walter Roach in a vicious nut-cracker. That play was good for 23 yards and a little groan went up from the Texans. Then John Hall went out.

You know the club was already short on wingbacks with Bob Harrell, Harold McClure and Pat Clifford on the bench with injured legs. Vic Montgomery had to go in for Johnny and that left only Lennon Blackmon in reserve for those wings.

Then Cotton Harrison went down with a leg injury and Big Bill Halls followed suit.

It certainly looked dark for the Frogs.

But the Frogs took time out and talked over this new flanker play. And they stopped it cold the rest of the afternoon. Harrison was able to return to the game later and Scotty McCall didn't need relief. After the Purple line got to functioning, the Broncs were helpless. They made some ground, of course, but were never able to drive the ball anywhere near scoring range.

143

But the Texans were in a hole most of the first quarter. Nello Falaschi intercepted on one of Sammy Baugh's slips and returned to the Frog 3-yard line before they got him from behind. But the Broncs couldn't make an inch running, and two passes into the end zone ended the threat.

Then early in the second chapter the Frog fans got a big scare. From his 47, Baugh launched a perfect pass to Roach. But the ball popped out of Roach's arms and fell into the hands of Seramin, a fast little back. The Bronco took off. Twice it appeared that he would be bagged but each time he broke free and continued his journey. Finally he raced across the goal untouched, but an alert official caught a Bronc blocker clipping on the Frog 14. Three plays made only three yards and then Pellegrini was rushed in to try a field goal from the 26-yard line.

It was miles short.

And that was the last serious Bronco threat. The Purple line halted the famous Santa Clara running game with four first downs. When the Broncs tried to pass in a pinch, the Purple secondary either knocked them down or intercepted. Montgomery, Roberts and Baugh got four enemy heaves and only one toss was completed by the foe.

That's defense.

The Frogs didn't have much luck running against the best line they've seen in many a moon but their passes did all right although the Broncs remained in a five-man line most of the afternoon. After Baugh found the range, he was just as deadly as ever. To say only that Baugh had those 40,000 fans cheering for him when the game ended would be gross understatement.

The winners scored with such suddenness that most of the crowd didn't know what was happening. Roberts, who played the game of his career, intercepted a Bronc pass on the Frog 15 and returned to the Purple 33.

After a shovel pass to Montgomery made two yards, Baugh rifled to Roach who made a great catch between two defenders. Roach flipped a back pass to Roberts, who carried to the Santa Clara 47.

Then Baugh called on an old favorite, a pass that scored twice on Baylor. It was a deep shot to McCall

behind the Bronco right half. The ball arched up perfectly and came down softly into Scott's arms on the Santa Clara 9. Again Baugh called a pass but his receivers were covered. So he tucked the ball under his arm and battled to the 5-yard line. Then Baugh dropped back and his famous arm uncoiled. In the end zone, Roach was traveling at full speed between secondary. The ball hit him like a bullet and he hugged it to his stomach for the touchdown. L.D. Meyer's point-after kick was high enough but to the left of the uprights.

That would have won for the Frogs but they weren't done. Baugh, who outpunted several Broncos all day, pushed the California boys into a hole early in the third stanza. A short return punt gave the Frogs the ball on the enemy 42. A shovel to McCall and a bullet pass to Roach made a new try on the Bronco 22. A shovel to McCall made nine steps but two other passes missed fire. Then Meyer stepped back and from the 21-yard line, arched a perfect boot through the posts. That kick would have been good from the 30- or 35-yard line. He really belted it.

Well, with those nine points, the Frogs went on defense. Baugh's fine punting held the foe at bay easily the rest of the game. Baugh was everything the southwest has been claiming for him. There wasn't a fan or sports writer who didn't know they had seen an All-American in action when this game was over.

And Roberts, Montgomery and McCall! That boy Scotty returned to his old high school form. He was tremendous.

Roach, Walls and Meyer were big standouts. Roach was easily the best wingman on the field. Ellis, Hale and Allie White turned in perfect games at the tackles.

But those guards and the center should really get the highest award of the god of courage. Cotton Harrison, Solon Holt, Bull Rogers and Ki Aldrich made a name for themselves in California today.

SCORE BY QUARTERS

TCU	6	3	0	0	—	9
Santa Clara	0	0	0	0	—	0

Frogs Stop Marquette, 16-6

By Flem Hall

Fort Worth Star-Telegram

DALLAS, Jan. 1, 1937

With a sling-bang attack that whipped over a field goal and two touchdowns in the first 25 minutes of play and with a sturdy defense that piled up the Marquette Golden Avalanche, Texas Christian University captured a spectacular football game New Year's Day. The score in the Cotton Bowl classic was 16-6.

So sudden, sharp and dazzling was the sweep of action of the battle that 15,000 spectators, who braved threatening weather, forgot the gray gloom of the afternoon.

Led by Sammy Baugh, who outpassed and outplayed "Buzz" Buivid to cinch his claim to the title of the greatest passer of the season, the Texans uncorked a flanking offense that flared into big gains both on the ground and in the air.

Although it was Baugh who paced the attack and won the attention of the crowd, it was L.D. Meyer who did the real damage to the cause of the Golden invaders from Milwaukee. He scored all of TCU's 16 points. He kicked a 33-yard field goal for the fist three points in the opening minutes. Before the first quarter had ended, he collaborated with Baugh on a 55-yard pass-and-run gain. In the second quarter he took an 18-yard heave from Vic Montgomery for the last score. He even converted after the first touchdown. His second attempt was blocked.

A 60-yard return of a punt by Art Guepe in the first quarter accounted for all of Marquette's points.

The game was played under almost perfect football conditions, and those timid souls who stayed away for fear of getting wet, or being bored with a mud battle will be eligible for a nice, life-long regret.

A drizzling rain that had fallen most of the day stopped 30 minutes before the 2 p.m. kickoff, and when the field covering was removed the grassless turf was dry and firm except for small and widely separated spots.

Agreeably surprised, the two great exponents of offensive football set out to celebrate by showing the folks something.

They did. Pulling the throttle wide open, they scored 16 points in the first 15 minutes. The premises were lathered with the old razz-mu-dazz in the most approved, unorthodox fashion.

The party cooled down after that. TCU scored again in the second period, but there was no scoring at all in the second half. The ball, however, continued at all times to move up and down the field with rare speed and quick exchange of possession.

Not only was Buivid overshadowed by Baugh for the day, but he was outsparkled by his teammate, Art Guepe. In addition to making the Marquette touchdown, the cocky little quarterback sparked the Golden Avalanche's attack all afternoon.

Before the game was half over Coach Dutch Meyer, feeling safe behind the 10-point lead, sent in most of his reserves. Every one of the 28 members of the squad (except Willie Walls, who was so ill he could not attend the

145

game) took part in the engagement. At no time after the first 25 minutes was the full first-string TCU team on the field. Baugh was on the bench for nearly a quarter and was only reinserted in the closing minutes when the crowd howled to see him one last time.

From start to finish the TCU line outcharged and outfought the smaller Marquette forwards. Cotton Harrison, Ki Aldrich, L.B. Hale, Forrest Kline, Solon Holt, Drew Ellis and Bull Rogers were most in evidence as Marquette plays were wrecked before they started and as big holes opened up for Frog ball carriers swinging around on reverses.

While the first string was on the field, TCU was in command of the game, but for a time in the third quarter, against the reserves. Marquette took the offensive. The Avalanche threatened twice, but each time the utility boys had the stuff to break up the drives and get the ball.

In the matter of passes completed, Marquette shaded TCU, 10-9, but the Frogs threw two for touchdowns, and gained more yards on theirs. Most of Buivid's were for short gains and not one of them did any real damage.

SCORE BY QUARTERS

TCU	10	6	0	0	—	16
Marquette	6	0	0	0	—	6

Halfback Harold McClure

Halfback Scott McCall

Fullback Glen Roberts

Purple Line, Blocking Top Notch

By Amos Melton
Fort Worth Star-Telegram

Admiral Dave Farragut was right. According to reliable sources, the Yankee skipper once opined that the best defense you can rig up is a fast and furious fire from your own guns.

The Frogs certainly proved the hypothesis here this afternoon.

The Golden Avalanche of Marquette had the offense as advertised — no question about it. Every time they got their hooks on the pig pelt, the boys from Lake Michigan did things with it.

They had the Purple fans right jittery.

But the Frogs knew what to do. It was obvious that when the Purple had the ball, the enemy couldn't do much. So the Frogs just went to work on offense. They had a real ground game here today. They ran for yards and yards against the generally orthodox Marquette defense.

And just to make it interesting, both Sammy Baugh and Davey O'Brien completed all kinds of passes.

In fact, for this game the Purple attack was nicely balanced between runs and passes. Marquette never knew what was coming and could never get set. Most critics left the field confident that if the Dutchman had left his first string in there all the way the Frogs would have run up 30 points.

The Purple line outplayed the Marquette forwards badly all day. They rushed the Avalanche passers to death. They smashed almost everything that came between the tackles. All of Marquette's ground was gained on sweepers — which worked so well because the Frog ends were dropped back with the flankers — and passes.

And on offense the Purple-clad line simply blocked the Hillstoppers off the field. At times there were holes six and eight yards wide in the visitors' line. Without doubt, the Frog blocking was the best of the season.

Harrison, Holt, Ellis, Meyer, Roach, Hale and Aldrich, the starting forwards, were great.

Allie White, Forrest Kline, Bull Rogers and Jack Tittle also played great ball when they went in.

This Aldrich is a hoss, that's all. And this lad Kline is going to be a great tackle.

Strangely enough, Sam Baugh had his greatest day as a runner in his last game. The tall boy really rambled for yards every time he got the ball. On the other hand, he had his poorest day punting. His first shot was straight to Art Guepe and resulted in the Avalanche touchdown. He didn't hit the ball well all day. Where last year in the Sugar Bowl game it was his great punting that won, today it was his passing and running.

And L. D. Meyer, the great little lad who has never really loved football, came into his own at last. It's doubtful if Willie Walls himself could have done as well as the 168-pounder from Waco, who closed out his string by scoring all of the Frogs' points. His field goal was perfect.

The angle was tough and the ball had to travel 32 yards. But his shot was perfectly in the middle and high enough to travel 10 more yards over the cross bar.

Sam and Edmonia on their wedding day in 1938.

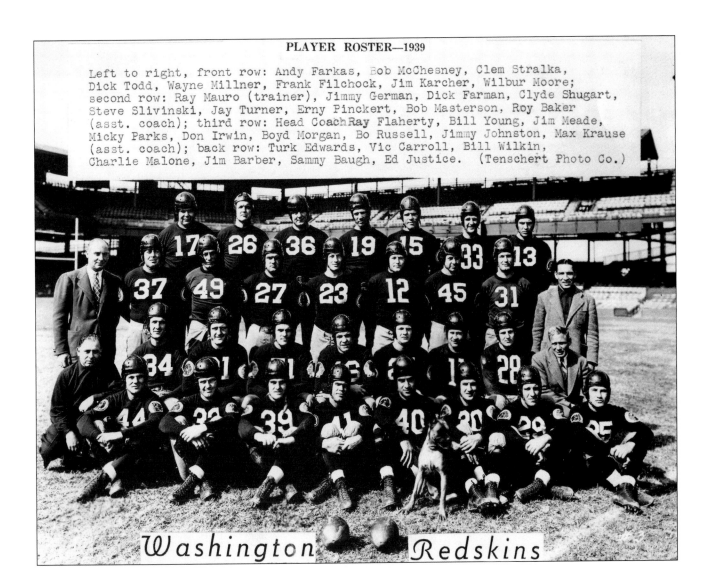

PLAYER ROSTER—1939

Left to right, front row: Andy Farkas, Bob McChesney, Clem Stralka,
Dick Todd, Wayne Millner, Frank Filchock, Jim Karcher, Wilbur Moore;
second row: Ray Mauro (trainer), Jimmy German, Dick Farman, Clyde Shugart,
Steve Slivinski, Jay Turner, Erny Pinckert, Bob Masterson, Roy Baker
(asst. coach); third row: Head Coach Ray Flaherty, Bill Young, Jim Meade,
Micky Parks, Don Irwin, Boyd Morgan, Bo Russell, Jimmy Johnston, Max Krause
(asst. coach); back row: Turk Edwards, Vic Carroll, Bill Wilkin,
Charlie Malone, Jim Barber, Sammy Baugh, Ed Justice. (Tenschert Photo Co.)

Washington *Redskins*

Baugh and two of his Redskins teammates, Andy Farkas (44) and Dick Todd (41).

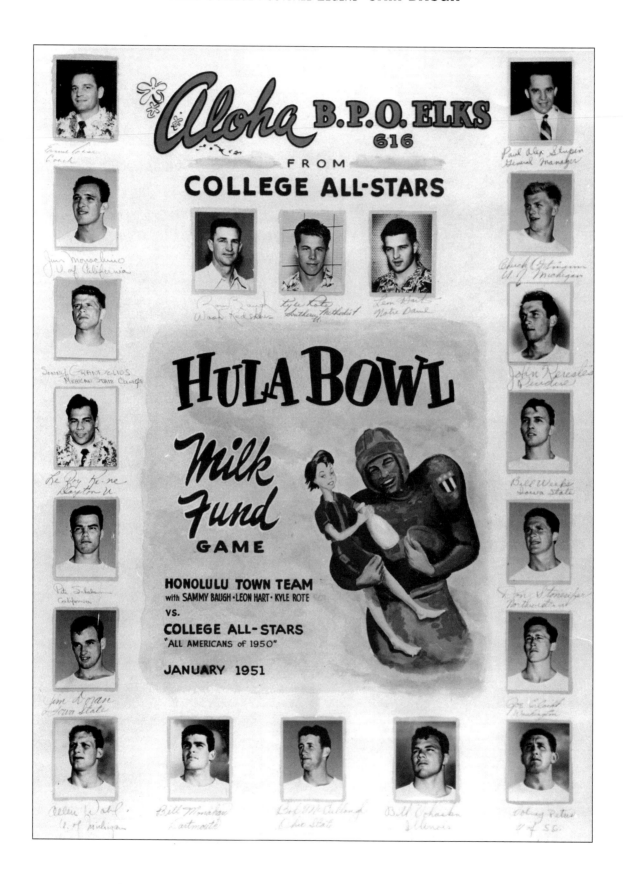

Baugh and New York Titans owner Harry Wismer at the Polo Grounds in 1959.

BIOGRAPHIES

ABOUT THE AUTHOR

Whit Canning is a sports writer with the *Fort Worth Star-Telegram*, where he has covered Southwest Conference and WAC football. He previously worked with the *Fort Worth Press*, covering the Southwest Conference and the Dallas Cowboys.

A native of Fort Worth and a graduate of Texas Christian University, this is his first book.

ABOUT THE EDITOR

Dan Jenkins is one of America's most renowned sports writers. Jenkins is the author of more than a dozen books, including the bestsellers, *Semi-Tough* (1972), *Dead Solid Perfect* (1974), *Limo* (1976), *Baja Oklahoma* (1981), *Life It's Own Self* (1984), *Fast Copy* (1988), and *You Gotta Play Hurt* (1991).

A native of Fort Worth and an alumnus of TCU, Jenkins' most enjoyable boyhood memories are having watched Sam Baugh and Davey O'Brien lead the Horned Frogs to national championships in 1935 and 1938.

CREDITS

Sam Baugh Collection: Front cover, *viii-ix*, 14, 20, 52, 61, 62, 64, 68, 76, 82, 84, 86, 92, 99, 100, 102, 104, 110, 111, 112, 150, 151, 152, 153, 154.

Bettmann Archives: *iii*, 26, 48, 95, 149.

Cotton Bowl: 57.

Fort Worth Star-Telegram Collection, University of Texas at Arlington Special Collections: Back cover, 54-55.

Dan Jenkins: 36, 119.

Sugar Bowl: *x*, *xi*, 130-131, 132, 133, 134.

TCU Sports Information: *iv*, *v*, *vi*, 17, 18, 19, 22, 23, 25, 29, 30, 31, 32, 34, 38, 41, 42, 44, 46, 51, 58-59, 67, 88, 107, 109, 120, 122, 124, 126-127, 129, 136-137, 139, 140, 142, 146-all.

Wide World Photo: 12-13, 71, 72-73, 74, 81, 89, 90-91, 94, 96, 114-115, 117, 155.